HITLER
THE VICTORY THAT
NEARLY WAS

HITLER
THE VICTORY THAT NEARLY WAS

Bruce Quarrie

GUILD PUBLISHING LONDON

This edition published 1989 by
Guild Publishing by
arrangement with
David & Charles Publishers plc

CN 6185

Typeset by ABM Typographics Limited, Hull
Printed in Great Britain by
Billings & Sons, Worcester
for David & Charles Publishers plc
Brunel House   Newton Abbot   Devon

Contents

Introduction

The academic scholar will say the 'what if?'s of history are an indulgence, that the 'what did happen' is far more important than the 'what might have happened'. They are, of course, right, in that it is what has actually happened which has created the world as we know it. Even so, I warrant that not one of them could truthfully say that he (or she) has not wondered what the course of English history might have been if William of Normandy's fleet had been decimated in a storm, as was the Spanish Armada five hundred years later; if Napoleon had been killed during the siege of Toulon or Winston Churchill at Omdurman; if . . . the list is endless, each new beginning creating an infinity of new possibilities.

The one man who dominates 20th century history is Adolf Hitler, born Alois Hiedler after some illegal namechanging in local records to an Austrian couple called Schickelgruber on 20 April 1889. And it is his conduct of the Second World War which concerns us here.

My own interest in the subject grew when, refighting some of the major battles of history as a wargamer, I came to appreciate how much of history relies on chance – the weather, a commander falling sick, a misconstrued order, even a chance love affair or a hangover! 'Wargaming' is often misunderstood. People see grown men moving model soldiers over a sculptured landscape, or counters on a map, and call it 'playing with toy soldiers'. So it can be, and the average child's game, or even that devised by the novelist H.G. Wells, are just that – games – which bear no resemblance to historical accuracy.

The true 'wargamer', on the other hand, studies his subject intensively. He learns the abilities and personal quirks of the leading military figures of his period. He learns about weapons' effectiveness: not just how far a rifle or cannon can fire, but how fast, with what penetration effect and accuracy, and at what rate. He even takes into account the comparative effectiveness of the same weapon in the hands of a newly trained conscript or a veteran of several campaigns. He studies how fast men can march – or in more modern times how fast tanks, ships, aircraft and missiles can move; what their endurance is – in other words, how long they can keep going without eating and drinking in the first place or refuelling and replenishing in the second; how much weight they can carry; the effectiveness of their armour protection, if any. He learns about logistics, lines of communication and supply, medical services, the techniques of siege warfare and a myriad other factors.

The point of all this is to guarantee that when he begins moving his model soldiers or counters he has almost, if not as good a knowledge of the tactics and capabilities of the 'troops' under his command as a Napoleon or Wellington, Montgomery or Rommel, had of his actual forces. Answering the 'why?' of wargaming is more difficult unless you play chess or a similar game of skill quite seriously. Indeed, wargaming has often been likened to 'chess with a thousand pieces', and certainly the pure 'game' itself forms a large part of the fascination. There is more to it than this, though. There is an equally great fascination in seeing the tactics of the time played out, the interraction between the different arms of service. Could such-and-such a battle have been won if one side had attacked on the left flank instead of the right, or vice versa? Or would the end result have been the same? Suppose it rained, so all movement on the battlefield was slowed down? Or suppose it had been fine instead of wet or snowing? Suppose the cavalry hadn't gone haring off after the loot in the enemy baggage train, but had remained on the field? Suppose. Just suppose.

This book could have begun with 'suppose Adolf Hitler had never been born', but that would not have left a great deal to write about . . . It could have started with him being killed in the First World War, when he won the Iron Cross as an infantry-man in the 16th Bavarian Regiment. It could have begun in 1923, when he was imprisoned following the Munich Beer Hall Putsch, an attempted takeover of the Bavarian government, and wrote *Mein Kampf* in his cell in Landsberg prison.

It was tempting to start the book in 1940 when the victorious Panzers overran France and the Low Countries and an invasion fleet was assembled to cross the English Channel, but there have been several books already about Operation 'Sealion' and whether it might or would not not have succeeded. It all hinged on the Luftwaffe's ability to destroy the Royal Air Force, and once Hitler and Göring switched their attention from Britain's airfields and radar stations to bomb the cities in reprisal for RAF attacks on the civilian population of Germany, the RAF gained the reprieve it so desperately needed. Even then, the attempt could very well have been resumed in the spring of 1941, but by that time Hitler's attention was focused on Russia and he was about to lead Germany into a disastrous war on two fronts. When the Japanese bombed Pearl Harbor later in the same year – crippling several capital ships but missing the vital aircraft carriers which were at sea at the time – Hitler gained an ally but, more importantly, an even more powerful enemy in the shape of the United States of America. From that point he could not win the war.

So backtrack. In September 1940 Italian forces invaded Egypt, then under British protection. The British Army trounced them and took thousands of prisoners. Hitler could not just abandon his ally Mussolini to such an ignominious fate, it reflected badly on the Axis alliance, so in February 1941 he sent one of his best Generals to Africa, Erwin Rommel, whose handling of the 7th Panzer Division in May and June the previous year had been exemplary. Together with a small contingent of German troops, Rommel amazed everybody by the skill and daring with which he reversed the Italian defeat and drove a shocked British Army back to where it had come from. Thus began a see-saw campaign along the North African coastline which lasted until 1943.

In the interim, Mussolini did it again. He invaded Greece, and his forces rapidly became hopelessly bogged down in the face of the tough little Greek army even before British forces intervened. Once again, Hitler had to come to the Duce's rescue, and the Balkan campaign delayed the planned invasion of Russia by a critical month or so, which meant that by the time German troops reached the outskirts of Moscow, winter was rapidly setting in and they were not equipped to fight a winter campaign. Another reason for the delay was that, having made his main thrust on Moscow, Hitler became diverted by the temptation of the Ukrainian grainfields, diverting a major part of his main striking force to achieve a resounding, but ultimately self-defeating, victory around Kiev.

After German troops defeated the Greeks and forced the Allied expeditionary force to evacuate to Crete, in May 1941 they launched a daring air and sea invasion of the island and after a short but very sharp campaign forced the Empire troops to evacuate again, this time to Egypt. These included General Bernard Freyberg's tough New Zealand Division. After the invasion of Crete, however, Hitler's attention was firmly focused on Russia and the Mediterranean theatre of operations became something of a sideshow as far as he was concerned. This left Rommel out on a limb because Allied warships and aircraft based on Malta inflicted crippling losses on his supply convoys. Now, if instead Hitler had gone through with an invasion of Malta, plans for which already existed, the whole situation in the eastern Mediterranean would have been totally different. This, therefore, is the starting point of this book, and the events which follow are, I believe, reasonable assumptions. The actual battles described, where they differ from 'real life', have been wargamed extensively to test their feasibility. However, it must be accepted that this is fiction, albeit documentary fiction closely based on fact, on available troop strengths, dates of introduction into service of new weapons, etc. Two major dates have been changed. The invasion of Russia is postponed from the summer of 1941 until the spring of 1942, when it would have stood an excellent chance of succeeding; and the Japanese are also persuaded to postpone their attack on Pearl Harbor. Both are acceptable 'what if?'s, and in turn generate their own logical sequences of probabilities.

The historical characters mentioned, such as Rommel, Guderian, Manstein, Freyberg, Auchinleck and so on are, obviously, real, and I do not believe I have attributed actions or reactions to them which would have been out of character. If anything in the book causes offence to their families I can only apologise in advance. Minor characters are entirely imaginary and any resemblance to any real person, living or dead, is purely coincidental. Where appropriate, I have provided notes to enable the reader to see what is factual and what is supposition. Obviously, my own interpretation of events will differ from those held by other people, since this book could have been written in any number of different ways. However, if it provides food for thought and enjoyment for the reader, I shall be well satisfied.

Bruce Quarrie
Wellingborough,
July 1988

The Pacific
War Zone
1942-43

RUSSIA

CHINA

KOREA

JAPAN

Vladivostock

Tokyo

Okinawa

Hong Kong

Phillipine
Islands

Bangkok

INDOCHINA

Saigon

MALAYA

Singapore

SUMATRA

BORNEO

Celebes

NEW
GUINE

JAVA

Timor

Darwin

AUSTRALIA

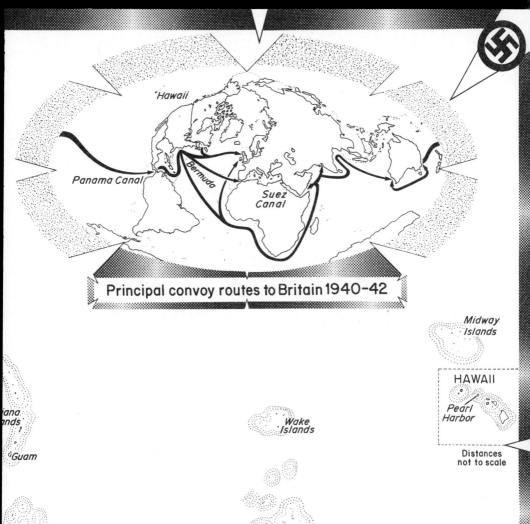

Principal convoy routes to Britain 1940-42

Hawaii

Panama Canal

Bermuda

Suez
Canal

Midway
Islands

HAWAII

Pearl
Harbor

Distances
not to scale

iana
nds

Guam

Wake
Islands

Gilbert
Islands

Solomon
Islands

Port
Moresby

Coral Sea

Samoa
Islands

Fiji Islands

8 Ⓐ 88

1
Bloodbath on Malta[1]

White. The sky and seemingly the very air radiated white. Major Walter Koch[2] squinted his eyes beneath the peak of his cap. The heat of the sun in September, before the rains, seemed to have evaporated the colour from the landscape, and even the olive and cypress trees were pale silhouettes against a greater brightness. Part of it was just dust, he realised, the all-pervasive white dust which made his scalp, neck and groin itch and failed to conceal the dark residue of sweat under his arms and down the length of the back of his faded tropical camouflage smock. But the greater part was the sheer white heat of the sun causing tunnel vision and nausea, the first sure signs of *Sonnenstich*[3]. Gratefully he entered the dim, cool taverna, and paused to allow his eyes to adjust. Good. Hans Jungwirt[4] was here, with three or four other more junior battalion officers. Hans, he was pleased to see, was drinking his rough red Cretan wine with iced water, but a couple of the others were already bleary at midday from too much foul-tasting retsina and ouzo. 'No action, that's the problem,' Koch thought as he joined the circle around the fly-encrusted table and shoved a filthy plate away to clear himself a place. The surly barkeeper gave it a perfunctory wipe with an equally dirty wet rag, rubbed it across his buttocks to dry it and slammed it beneath the counter.

'Herr Major?', Hans asked. 'Milk,' Koch replied, wiping his forehead and brushing back the thinning strands of his hair, once dark but now bleached almost as white as the landscape itself. He had never liked the drink as a child but now the tart goat's milk of Greece and, more recently, Crete was almost all he ever drank. He picked up a discarded olive and shivered suddenly in the comparative cool.

'Who knows anything about Hercules?', he asked conversationally.

There was a predictable and perplexed silence. Young Dietrich looked anxious to answer but was obviously waiting for one of his more senior companions to speak first. 'One of the Greek gods?' ventured Yuri Hermann, the Sudeten Czech in the company. 'Almost right,' said Koch, turning his gaze to Dietrich. 'He was the greatest of the old Greek heroes,' the youngster said, practically blushing. 'Cleaned out the Aegean stables and killed someone because he didn't get his reward, caught a sacred bull somewhere here on Crete I think, fought a monster in Africa, that sort of thing. I seem to remember he was poisoned in the end.'

'Close enough,' said Koch, 'but from next week the word will mean something else, especially to the *Amis*.' The thirty-year-old veteran, hero of Eben Emael and Maleme, leaned forward conspirationally. 'It's Malta,' he added quietly, although in truth there was little chance of being overheard. 'We'll be shipping out within the next couple of days.' The men stirred and glanced at each other. Dietrich turned pale but Hermann's eyes flashed. Jungwirt's face just went blank as he absent-mindedly polished his sand goggles with the white silk scarf around his neck, for as second in command of the 1st Battalion, *Luftlande-Sturm-Regiment*, he knew the amount of work Koch's simple words were going to mean for him in particular.

'*Herkule*'[5] was the codename assigned by the OKW, the German General Staff, to the planned airborne and amphibious invasion of Malta. The island was a bogeyman to the German forces in the Mediterranean. First bombed by the Italian Regia Aeronautica on 11 June 1940, the day after Koch's own specially-formed assault group had landed its gliders on the roof of the supposedly impregnable Belgian fortress of Eben Emael, it had resisted every assault by both the German and Italian air forces ever since, just as the islanders, led by the Knights Hospitallers, had held out against the Turks during the great siege of 1565. Lying only sixty miles to the south of Sicily, this tiny island barely seventeen miles long by nine wide and with a population of a mere 250,000, had been part of the British Empire since 1814 when its inhabitants had asked for the Crown's protection after throwing out a French expeditionary force during the Napoleonic Wars. It had been extensively fortified over the years, its limestone structure providing the raw material for great walls and ramparts as well as houses and seemingly innumerable churches. It was this construction which had largely saved the islanders so far in the Second World War, for the solid limestone blocks were impervious to incendiary bombs and gave very effective protection against high explosive blast. Caves served as natural air raid shelters and tunnels were hewn out of the living rock to provide others. When the Italian bombers came over you might have almost thought the island was solely populated by dogs.

Despite the fact that the Italian fleet was one of the largest and most modern in the world, since its humiliating defeats by Admiral Sir Andrew Cunningham at the battle of Calabria in July 1940, at Taranto in November and off Cape Matapan in March 1941, it had largely skulked in harbour, only its submarines venturing out to attack the vital convoys which kept the island supplied. Contrary to popular opinion, as Koch well knew because he had several friends in the Italian armed forces, this was not due to any lack of courage on the part of individual Italian sailors, but to low morale produced by appallingly inept leaders. 'And that includes Mussolini,' he thought. If *Il Duce* had not attacked Greece earlier in the year and *Der Führer* had not opted to help him win a campaign which was going disastrously wrong, Walter Koch and his lads would, he was sure, have been well on the road to Moscow. Russia was the main enemy, the permanent threat to European unity. It had been clever of Hitler to share the spoils of Poland with Stalin and sign that tongue-in-cheek 'non-aggression' treaty, but he and most of his friends knew where the danger – and the opportunities – lay. It was not on this heat-sink of a verminous Greek island which had only been secured at such cost in May – nearly a third of the original 22,000 German *Fallschirmjäger* (paratroops) dead or wounded; nor was it on *'Festung* Malta', although Koch appreciated that the subjugation of Russia relied upon General Rommel's victory in North Africa, and that while the Royal Air Force and the Fleet Air Arm still retained Malta, German shipping convoys to the 'Desert Fox' would continue to suffer greater losses than the *Wehrmacht* could sustain.

'A pretty pickle,' he mused, as he returned his attention to the buzz of speculation which now surrounded him. If Crete had been a tough nut to crack, Malta, with its far more formidable terrain and defences, was going to be a nightmare. He was right, but victory was also to give Germany the key to the Mediterranean.

As the clouds of war gathered during the late 1930s the British had strengthened their garrison on Malta, which the Royal Navy if no-one else realised was the key to Mediterranean strategy. The visually impressive but technologically 19th century fortifications were modernised and extra artillery batteries, particularly of anti-aircraft guns, were installed, although not in the quantities really needed*; and as the last remaining months of peace ticked away the Grand Harbour was full of warships. Then, suddenly, they were gone, called away to carry the war to the enemy, and the island's main towns became strangely silent as all those of the civilian population who could be persuaded to leave vacated the area of the harbour and the docks and the narrow twisting streets of Valetta, Vittoriosa, Cospicua and Senglea. Many moved to Malta's sister island, Gozo, which, possessing no military installations, was not expected to be attacked. The street hawkers with their birds, their strong goats' cheeses and other local wares were absent too, but the churches and bars were full, while bread – as in England – was still not rationed; but everyone carried a gasmask.

For a while, though, the island basked in an unreal peace, the skies clear apart from the half dozen obsolete Gloster Sea Gladiator biplanes of the Hal Far Fighter Flight[6] which formed its sole aerial defence. Even they were an accident, Fleet Air Arm leftovers discovered still crated scant weeks before the onslaught began and hastily assembled, for Royal Air Force had originally deemed the island indefensible so had provided no defence. Meanwhile, in a grimy bar in Rethymnon on an island at the eastern end of the Mediterranean, German paratroop officers discussed the same subjects.

They talked about the mauling the lumbering torpedo-carrying Swordfish biplanes of Britain's Fleet Air Arm had administered on the Italian fleet at Taranto nearly a year ago; they

*The original plan had been for 112 heavy and sixty light AA guns plus 24 searchlights, but at the outbreak of war only the searchlights, 34 heavy (3.7- and 4.5-inch) and a meagre eight light (40 mm) guns had arrived. By September 1941, however, these had been greatly increased and were giving the German and Italian bombers a real mauling.

worried about the arrival of Hawker Hurricane fighters on the
island for, while no one-to-one match for the Luftwaffe's Messerschmitt Bf 109s, they were making the Italians wary of attacking by day; they talked about the British Navy and what a
disaster the amphibious side of the invasion of Crete had been
due to the intervention of a mere three cruisers and four destroyers; they worried over the losses the German and Italian
convoys to Rommel were suffering from English aircraft and
submarines – apparently 35 per cent of their ships had been
sunk in the last month, according to a confidential report Koch
had discussed with Jungwirth, and it looked as though the toll
was mounting; they knew from Luftwaffe intelligence that the
British had a radar installation on the north of the island so
their approach would not long remain undetected; and above
all they talked about the problems the rugged Maltese terrain
was going to cause parachutists and gliders.

The only reasonable landing areas were the airfields of Hal
Far, Ta'Qali and Luqa and the aircraft dispersal sites at Safi,
Mqabba and Qrendi, but these of course had the heaviest defences outside the naval harbour. Moreover, the forlorn collection of Gladiators, which had gone down in British mythology
as a trio named 'Faith', 'Hope' and 'Charity', had been super-
seded not just by the Hurricanes, but by naval Fulmars,
Swordfish torpedo attack aircraft and Blenheim bombers,
which had commenced plastering Sicily earlier in the year.
(There had been some Wellingtons and Sunderland flying
boats too, but the ferocity of *Fliegerkorps X*'s attacks had forced
their evacuation to Egypt in March.) The remainder of the island, where it did not consist of steep limestone crags, lonely
trees and thornbrush, was patterned in tiny fields with ancient
drystone walls, and even these had now been filled by British
soldiers with sharp stakes and keen wires to impale or decapi-
tate any invaders from the sky. Malta in September 1941 was
not, therefore, the relatively defenceless target it had been a
year earlier, Koch confided to his subordinates.

It had never been his policy to hide unpleasant truths. Some
commanders preferred to keep their men in ignorance, but
Koch believed that soldiers fought better if their eyes were
open to the obstacles, and could react more quickly and sensi-
bly to sudden crises. There was an intelligence risk, of course,
which was why the sort of frank conversation he was having

was frowned upon by the *Feldgendarmerie* and the bastards of the SD, the *Sicherheitsdienst* or SS security people. But in 1941 a Knights Cross holder did not worry about such vermin, and Koch spoke freely to the men upon whose shoulders largely lay responsibility for success or failure in at least one phase of the forthcoming operation.

General Erwin Rommel had arrived in Tripoli on 12 February 1941 to bolster the Italian forces in North Africa which had received such a trouncing at the hands of Generals Wavell and O'Connor. With just two divisions to begin with, the 5th *Leichte* and the 15th *Panzer*, he had advanced rapidly, retaking Benghazi, Bardia and Sollum in April (capturing General O'Connor in the process), defeated a spirited counter-attack in June and laid siege to Tobruk. But to advance further into Egypt he desperately needed a greater and more regular flow of supplies, particularly of fuel, ammunition and spare parts for his tanks which were continuously breaking down due to the heat, sand and sheer number of miles they were being forced to drive. British submarines and destroyers, of which eight and four respectively were now permanently based on Malta, had been exacting a terrible toll on the Italian convoys despite the protection of the Regia Aeronautica and *Fliegerkorps X*. Malta was the thorn in Rommel's flank and he had flown to Rastenburg on 26 July for a stormy meeting with Hitler to demand action.

Der Führer was initially reluctant to contemplate an airborne invasion after the grievous losses the *Fallschirmjäger* had suffered on Crete two months earlier, but General Kurt Student – the founding father of the paratroops – believed it could be done, especially if the dormant Vichy French fleet in Toulon could sail to lure the Royal Navy away. Eventually persuaded, Hitler had instructed the OKW to prepare a feasibility study, and from this had emerged the plan for Operation 'Herkule'.

Despite the fact that its garrison was smaller than the British Empire forces had been on Crete, Malta as a target for invasion posed tremendous problems. Its interior was inhospitable apart from the half dozen airstrips. Its western coast was particularly rugged, with cliffs rising to a sheer 400 feet and beyond them a range of hills blocking access to the more heavily populated southern and eastern areas. Because of this the east

coast, especially around Valletta and the Grand Harbour, was
heavily defended with coastal gun batteries which, while of relatively small calibre and short range (mainly 6 and 25 pdrs),
would inflict a great deal of damage on any landing barges
heading inshore. There was also the Malta Striking Force to
contend with (the destroyers and submarines mentioned earlier). The ideal place for an amphibious landing would have
been Marsaxlokk Bay on the south-eastern corner of the island,
adjacent to Hal Far and within quick striking distance of Luqa
and Valetta, but this was also heavily mined and defended. The
only other suitable places for amphibious landings were Mel-
lieha or St Paul's Bays, both on the north-east coast and relatively lightly defended. However, the nearest airfield to these
was Ta'Qali in the centre of the island, close to the ancient capital city of Mdina, which itself was heavily fortified. Thus the
airborne troops at Luqa, and especially those at Hal Far, would
be separated by almost the whole length of the island from
their amphibious support, and the island roads were for the
most part merely dusty cart tracks.

('No *Baedeckers!*', Koch warned his companions. Friedrich-
August von der Heydte, commander of the 3rd Regiment's 1st
Battalion, had blotted his copy book before Crete by buying one
of these popular guides in an Athens bookstore. 'Oh,' the girl
assistant had said innocently, 'You're going to Crete . . .')[7]

In the end a compromise was reached. No attempt would be
made to seize Hal Far from the air. Instead a massed air raid by
Italian Savoia-Marchetti SM.79s and German Ju 87s and '88s
would strike there as well as over Valetta and Marsaxlokk to
keep the defenders occupied. These would also draw off most of
the British fighters, it was hoped. The bombers would approach
at their normal altitude of around 12,000 feet. They would be
followed by the Ju 52 paratroop transports which would fly at a
mere couple of hundred feet to minimise the chances of radar
detection, only rising to a minimum height for parachute jumping (350 to 400 feet) just before they crossed the coastline. (A
low altitude drop had been decided upon both to help in avoiding radar detection and to prevent the wide dispersal of troops
all over the landscape which had produced such heavy casualties on Crete and nearly spelled disaster for the whole operation.) Ju 52s would also tow the DFS 230 gliders forming the
third wave of the assault, each containing more men and a few

items of heavy support equipment, such as 2.8 cm *Panzerbüchse* 41 tapered-bore anti-tank and 7.5 cm Rheinmetall lG40 recoilless guns.

The main force of the aerial armada was to land at Luqa and its three satellite airstrips, because it was known to be most heavily defended and was closer to Valletta and Hal Far than Ta'Qali. The men landed there knew they would have to hold out until their comrades at the more northerly airfield were reinforced by the amphibious troops landed in St Paul's Bay and could begin pressing forward. Walter Koch was both proud and apprehensive at the fact that his battalion was one of those selected for the assault on Luqa itself, because of its experience at Maleme. He, personally, had received a mild head wound there scant minutes after landing, and he plucked at the scar as he continued to brief his team. Although a formal briefing would follow, he wanted them to go prepared with at least the bare essentials of knowledge.

Certainly Koch thought the plan was better than that originally proposed by Field Marshal Albert Kesselring, which had called for a parachute drop supported by bombers on the high ground to the south-west of the island coupled with a naval assault on Valletta itself and a diversionary raid against Marsaxlokk Bay. This would have dropped the *Fallschirmjäger* close to the main enemy forces and in grossly unsuitable terrain which would have caused dozens of unecessary injuries upon landing.

To distract Royal Naval forces in the western Mediterranean, the French battleship *Richelieu* would sail with a convoy of destroyers from Toulon towards Oran, in Algeria. Her mission was sacrificial, purely that of a decoy, and she would be unable to fight back if attacked for she would only carry a skeleton crew of volunteers. Once her sailing was detected and British warships known to be heading towards her, she would turn smartly back towards Toulon. If she was sunk, she was sunk, but the OKW estimated, probably correctly, that the British would find a target so tempting more irresistible than any ordinary convoy. Meanwhile, the Italian Navy would provide more suitable transport for the amphibious side of the operation than the Greek fishing boats which had been used during Operation '*Merkur*' ('Mercury'), the invasion of Crete.

The forces to be assembled on Sicily for the new operation

were the battle-hardened veterans of Crete apart from all the new faces which had replaced those men fallen in the earlier operation or who had transferred to other units. The *Luftlande-Sturm-Regiment* in which Walter Koch commanded the 1st Battalion, would be in the third wave of the assault. The regiment's overall commander was Generalmajor Eugen Meindl, and its 2nd, 3rd and 4th Battalions were led respectively by Majors Edgar Stentzler, Horst Trebes (promoted from Oberleutnant after Major Scherber was killed) and Walter Gericke. The first wave would comprise the three regiments of the 7th *Flieger* Division, commanded now by Richard Heidrich, pro moted to the rank of Generalmajor for his role in the Cretan operation after its original commander, General Wilhelm Süssmann, had also been killed. His three regimental commanders were Obersts Bruno Bruer, Alfred Sturm and Ludwig Heilmann (another promotion) respectively. Each regiment was of three battalions. The 1st Battalion, 1st *Fallschirmjäger* Regiment (I/FJR 1) was led by Major Erich Walther, the second (II/FJR 1) by Major Harry Herrmann and the third (III/FJR 1) by Major Karl Schulz. I/FJR 2 was commanded by Major Hans Kroh, II/FJR 2 by Major Erich Pietzonka and III/FJR 2 by Major Josef Barmetler; while I/FJR 3 was led by Major Freiherr von der Heydte, II/FJR 3 by Major Karl Becker and III/FJR 3 by Major Hans Lehmann, who had now stepped into Heilmann's shoes.

The division chosen to undertake the amphibious side of the operation was General Julius 'Papa' Ringel's equally tough 5th *Gebirgsjäger* (Mountain) Division, the General having recovered from the wound he sustained on Crete. This was much stronger than either of the airborne formations, comprising two infantry regiments, the 85th and 100th, an artillery regiment (the 95th) and supporting motor cycle, pioneer, anti-tank and reconnaissance battalions. The 85th Infantry Regiment would be flown in by Ju 52s to reinforce Ta'Qali after the paras had secured it and the 100th to Luqa, so only the support troops and their heavier equipment would voyage by sea. The total force was just under 20,000 men, ten per cent less than had taken part in Operation '*Merkur*', but more than sufficient to overwhelm Malta's defences if the Royal Navy did not intervene in strength. Had the aircraft carrier *Illustrious*, in particular, been still on station the operation would have been suicidal, but she had been crippled by the Luftwaffe earlier in the year and was still being repaired at Alexandria.

What of the opposition? The British Army's troops on the island amounted to the equivalent of a brigade; indeed, at this time it was called the 1st Malta Brigade, overall CO being Colonel Ivan de la Bere. Luqa was principally defended by the 1st Battalion, Royal Hampshire Regiment, under Lieutenant-Colonel H.C. Westmoreland, and was based in the nearby village of Gudja. Lt-Colonel Edward J. Newall's 1st Battalion, Cheshire Regiment (a machine-gun unit) was in Vittorosia, overlooking the Grand Harbour, with detachments at Luqa; the 1st Dorsets under Lt-Colonel A.T. Grimley were to their south, in Zabbar. The 2nd Battalion, Royal West Kent Regiment, commanded by Lt-Colonel Arthur Bonham-Carter was in Quormi, practically in the centre of the island and directly on the route the *Gebirgsjäger* and paras from Ta'Qali would have to take to relieve their comrades at Luqa. The 2nd Devonshires, led by Lt-Colonel A.W. Valentine (who was inevitably nicknamed 'Cupid' by his troops), were furthest from what would be the main scenes of action, at Zejtun near the southwest coast, adjacent to Marsaxlokk Bay.

These, however, were not the only defenders, for there were many Royal Artillery, Royal Engineers and Royal Signals troops, plus of course the King's Own Malta Regiment, the Royal Malta Artillery and the Home Guard (known formerly as the Malta Volunteer Defence Force). However, the total strength of the armed defenders (excluding the police, air raid wardens and Passive Defence Force – which built many of the pillboxes, tank traps and barbed wire obstacles as well as air raid shelters) only numbered some 10-11,000 men, of whom less than half were properly-trained regulars.

For the most part Malta's Governor, Lieutenant-General William Dobbie, relied on the anti-aircraft and coastal defence batteries – of which there were many – to defend the island from invasion; as well, of course, as on the Royal Navy. All had sweated through a seemingly endless long, hot summer, longing for the cooling September rains and besieged it seemed by the elements as much as by the enemy. In total there were four heavy anti-aircraft regiments, two British and two Maltese, each of six troops with four guns apiece; and four light anti-aircraft regiments, three British and one Maltese, each of nine troops with six guns apiece. These batteries revelled under un-pronounceable names such as Tal-Qrogg, Xrobb il-Ghagin and Bizbizija, even though it was noticeable that the Maltese people had largely adopted English words for the weapons of modern war, such as 'fighter' instead of *ajruplan tal-glied*!

In the air, Ta'Qali was principally a Hurricane field for the aircraft of 126 and 249 Squadrons, Luqa for the Blenheims and few remaining Wellingtons of 105 and 107 Squadrons and Hal Far the Hurricanes of 185 Squadron and Swordfish and Mary-lands of 830 Squadron, Fleet Air Arm. Aircraft numbers total-led 69 Hurricanes, eighteen Blenheims, seventeen Wellingtons, twelve Swordfish and seven Marylands, a total of 123 service-able machines – half the strength of *Fliegerkorps X*, which it-self was to be reinforced by *Fliegerkorps II* for Operation '*Her-kule*'. The island's aerial defence was the charge of Air Vice-Marshal Hugh Lloyd.

The secret weapon upon which all the British and Maltese hopes would ride or fall was an invisible one: Ultra. The Secret Intelligence Service, otherwise known as MI6, had earlier in the year succeeded in cracking the German Enigma codes through the use of a captured machine purloined by Polish in-telligence and an early, semi-mechanical computer called 'The Bombe'. The German armed forces used their Enigma coding machines, which resembled a pair of typewriters in tandem, to transmit all their operational orders. From the time the codes had been finally deciphered, therefore, the British had known every German move beforehand. They had known almost all the operational details of Operation '*Merkur*', yet Crete fell de-spite the fact the defenders were forewarned and outnumbered the invaders by two to one.

Two factors prevented the work of the Ultra scientists at Bletchley Park, in Bedfordshire, from being as effective as it might in defeating the Germans with relative ease. Many in high command believed that Crete was not important, and should be sacrificed. Moreover, if General Bernard Freyberg, commanding the Empire troops on the island, had been given the full facts, he would have redeployed accordingly to meet the threat. And that, inevitably, would have revealed to the Germans that there was a colossal leak somewhere in their security, something which the enemy could not have learned by traditional means. This is where intelligence can become a truly double-edged sword. To take advantage of one situation can mean sacrificing a greater, possibly unforseen, victory later; and winning a single battle does not mean victory in a war.

Of course, valuable though it was, Ultra could not reveal *everything*. Written messages sent by teleprinter landlines could not be intercepted, nor those delivered by despatch riders, nor those issued verbally. Thus, while MI6 knew the Germans were preparing a sizeable force of ships and aircraft, and concentrating some of their best troops on Sicily, they did not know their objective – and at this stage of the war all the signs pointed to reinforcements for Rommel in the desert. The fact that the concentration seemed to be centred on Messina added further weight to this conviction, for the port opened on to a direct, short, straight line route to Benghazi. The additional fact that the Luftwaffe and Regia Aeronautica seemed to be tapering off their bombardment of Malta also drew attention away from the island, for surely they would have stepped it up instead if they had been preparing an invasion? Thus were the boffins defeated, in a way, by their own science.

British warships in the eastern Mediterranean were alerted to a probable troop convoy sailing from Messina to Benghazi early in September. Then a high-altitude PRU (Photographic Reconnaissance Unit) Spitfire from Gibraltar brought electrifying news. Photographs taken on a routine sortie over the Vichy French naval base at Toulon on 5 September showed that the battleship *Richelieu* was being readied for sea. The *Richelieu* was one of France's two most modern, fast and powerful battleships (the other being the *Jean Bart*). Laid down in 1935 and completed in 1940, she had a displacement of 47,548 tons, was 813 feet in length and had a main armament of eight fifteen-inch guns. Her normal crew complement was 1,550 men and her four steam turbine engines gave her a top speed of over thirty knots. With a scratch crew and no ammunition aboard, her displacement would come down to around 43,000 tons and her speed would go up. The Royal Navy had unsuccessfully tried to destroy her at Dakar in July 1940 but she had escaped back to France where her mere presence was a constant menace to British Mediterranean convoys. The news was flashed to Admiral Sir James Somerville, commander of the famous Force 'H' which comprised the battleships *Nelson*,

Rodney and *Prince of Wales* together with the aircraft carrier
Ark Royal. Force 'H' had been responsible for providing escort
to the various Malta convoys during the summer of 1941, accompanied by Rear Admiral Harold Burrough's Force 'X' of five
cruisers and nine destroyers. At the time the news arrived both
forces were in Gibraltar preparing to sail with another convoy,
codenamed 'Halberd', later in the month. All leave was cancelled while the RAF despatched a low-level Spitfire to confirm
the evidence in the first photos on the 6th.

At the same time, at the other end of the Mediterranean the
German airborne and mountain troops who had been resting
on Crete also had their leave stopped and prepared to embark
for Sicily in three Italian liners which had been converted into
troopships, the *Marco Polo, Victoria* and *Esperia*[8]. They would
have a strong escort of destroyers while the Regia Aeronautica
and Luftwaffe would provide continuous daylight air cover for
the 440-mile voyage, which would take just over a day to complete. Weapons were cleaned and oiled, last-minute souvenirs
purchased, and the men boarded their vessels at dusk. The convoy would not set sail until 2 am, however, so that its departure
would hopefully remain undetected and, more importantly, the
last part of its voyage, when it would be most vulnerable to air
attack from Malta, would also be covered under the protection
of darkness.

The three ships and their escorts slid stealthily out of the
harbour in the still of the early hours of 7 September and by the
time the sky was lightening four hours later they were over
fifty miles away. The strictest radio silence was observed. At
6:32 am a lone Focke-Wulf Fw 200 Condor maritime reconnaissance aircraft out of Greece spotted them, circled once and
turned back towards its base. An hour later a flock of tiny
specks at 18,000 feet resolved themselves through binoculars
into a squadron of Bf 109 fighters; throughout the rest of the
day, until darkness fell again shortly before 9 pm, the squadrons relieved each other at intervals of about three-quarters of
an hour, for the aircraft's endurance was only just over two
hours. Fortunately for the convoy the skies remained clear
apart from this reassuring presence and the ships proceeded
placidly across the glittering Ionian Sea. As dusk fell ships'
officers checked thoroughly throughout their vessels for any
porthole which might unwarily have been left open and so emit

a chink of light to betray their presence. Most of the troops stayed out on the decks, lifejackets to hand, eagerly breathing in the cooling air after the furnace of the day. Even though they knew rationally that talking would not reveal their presence to the enemy, most spoke seldom and then in low voices. Trails of phosphorescence from the wakes of the ever-circling destroyers created strange nebulae of sea stars around them. All gun and depth charge crews were fully alert but still nothing disturbed the air or the sea. Tension mounted as they approached the Strait of Messina but there were no untoward incidents and the convoy slipped undetected into Messina harbour itself just as the false dawn began illuminating the sky.

Hans Jungwirt lit the pipe which he had unconsciously been sucking for the past hour. 'So far, so good, Walter,' he remarked quietly. Koch nodded agreement. 'The next bit's going to be rather tougher, though,' he said.

The airborne troops disembarked at dawn and clambered into their waiting trucks. The *Luftlande-Sturm-Regiment* was destined for Calabria, for its gliders needed a decent concrete runway from which to take off; this airfield also housed the Junkers Ju 88s of KG 606 and 806[9] (KG – *Kampfgeschwader* = bomber wing) and 1/NJG 2 (NJG –*Nachtjagdgeschwader* = night fighter wing). The 7th *Flieger* Division went to Palermo and Trapani on the north side of the island where they joined the Italian 2nd *Folgore* Division, itself a paratroop formation which had been trained by Bernhard Ramcke[10], one of the Luftwaffe's most experienced and energetic officers. This division was being held in reserve to reinforce the German troops on Malta if needed. Palermo and Trapani's normal contingent of Ju 88s of 1/KG 54 and 2 and 3/KG 77 had vacated the airfields and moved to Gerbini and Comiso. (The squadrons of shorter-ranged Ju 87 Stukas of 1, 2 and 3/St.G 3 (St.G – *Stukageschwader* = Stuka wing) and Erpr.G 1 (Erpr.G – *Erprobungsgruppe* = experimental group), together with the Bf 109 fighters of 2/JG 3 (JG – *Jagdgeschwader* = fighter wing) and 1, 2 and 3/JG 53 and the Bf 110s of 2/ZG 26 (ZG – *Zerstörergeschwader* = 'destroyer', or heavy fighter wing), were all based at Comiso and other more southerly airfields such as Cassibile, Gela and Biscari.) The men of the 5th *Gebirgsjäger* Division remained aboard ship, luxuriating in the extra space now the paras had moved out, although there were the expected grumbles about no shore leave.

The Germans were unable to fully conceal their preparations from the Royal Air Force, but they intended to hide their extent as much as possible from any British agents in Messina.

The next 24 hours saw a hive of activity on Sicily, but on Malta there was an eerie calm – the proverbial calm before the storm, in fact, but that could only be seen with hindsight. The Ju 88s and Breda 20s of the *Regia Aeronautica*'s 37° *Stormo* made their usual nightly attack on the 8th, hitting Valletta yet again and losing two aircraft to anti-aircraft fire, but the daytime was unbroken. The following night was silent, and the long-suffering Maltese looked upwards and listened with mixed relief and apprehension at the almost unprecedented break in the Luftwaffe's routine. What was going on? Dawn of the 10th provided the answer.

Church bells began to clamour and sirens wail on Malta while it was still dark at 5 am, the RAF radar station on the north coast having detected the leading wave of Ju 88s soon after they crossed the Sicilian coast, still climbing to their operational altitude. While civilians scurried bleary-eyed to their shelters, gun crews stood-to. At Ta'Qali and Hal Far duty pilots scrambled their Hurricanes — twelve from each. The off-duty aircrew, roused from their beds, hurried to don their boots, flying jackets and Mae Wests and ran out to the dispersal areas where ground crews were starting to warm up the engines of the other machines: the Swordfish, Blenheims and Wellingtons would head to safety out at sea, there to circle until recalled when the 'all clear' was radioed to them. Aboard the four warships in Grand Harbour – the light cruisers HMSs *Aurora* and *Penelope*, under Captains W.G. Agnew and A.D. Nichol, and the destroyers *Lance* and *Lively* under Lieutenant-Commanders R.W.F. Northcott and W.F.E. Hussey – klaxons squawked their urgent summons and gun crews donned their anti-flash gear before racing along the companionways to their stations. In the Governor's Residence General William Dobbie strode to his command centre in the basement.

Shortly the drone of approaching aero engines could be heard then the bombers could be seen, their wings catching the sunlight at 12,000 feet which had not yet reached the ground. The first wave droned menacingly past Valletta while its escorting Messerschmitts dove eagerly to meet the ascending Hurricanes. Within moments a ferocious dogfight had begun, sprawling over the centre of the island, contrails bright in the clear dawn air, while bombs began to rain on and around Hal Far. Wave after wave the bombers came, the Ju 88s joined by Italian SM.79s, and now the bombs began to fall around the battered buildings and high stone walls of Valletta and the harbour. Anti-aircraft guns pounded from the warships and the shore batteries and dark puffs of smoke exploded around the bombers, seemingly without effect at first. Then one aircraft fell away from the formation, trailing smoke from its port engine, and disappeared out towards the sea. There was no jubilation amongst the gunners, just the slam and recoil of the breech, the clang of ejected shell cases, the sweat to reload as quickly as possible, the urgent necessity to fire, fire and fire again overriding all other considerations.

And still the bombers came, and more fighters to engage the Hurricanes, while the crunch of bombs, the hammering of the heavy artillery, the sharper crack of the Bofors and pompoms and the rattle of machine-gun fire blended into a hellish cacophony.

At Ta'Qali and Luqa the anti-aircraft gunners were as busy as elsewhere, but the fact that no bombs were dropping around them from the huge aerial armada overhead did cause puzzlement. The troops who had dived for slit trenches or shelters when the sirens had sounded peered skywards apprehensively. Those in the Watch Offices and Ops Rooms knew Hal Far was taking a pounding, yet so far *they* had not been attacked. What devilry was the Luftwaffe up to this time? The answer was not long in coming: an almost hysterical telephone call from the radar station reported Ju 52 transport aircraft in large numbers approaching at low level over the coast, preceded by Me 110s. Invasion! It was the only answer . . . but how could it be combatted? The Hurricanes were already totally involved in the overhead mêlée, and all the other aircraft were miles away – for what good they might have been in a dogfight. Ta'Qali was almost defenceless apart from its anti-aircraft guns and machine-gun posts. Luqa was in slightly better state, and frantic word of the approach of the lumbering troop transports was rushed to Colonel Westmoreland of the Hampshires. Plans against the possibility of invasion had, of course, been devised months ago, and the battalion's soldiers poured out of their shelters at the strident, repeated, four bugle notes which

warned of an imminent airborne landing, running like berser-
kers for their sandbagged positions. The problem at Luqa was
that there was not just the one airfield, there were four – the
main one and the three dispersal sites linked by trackways
made of petrol cans beaten flat which shimmered under the rising sun. Westmoreland swore uncharacteristically.

The news reached General Dobbie at the same time, but he
was forced to hesitate. He could not order the Dorsets or Kents
to move until he was sure where the invasion was going to be
centred, while the Cheshires and Devons could not move in any
case for the hail of high explosive and shrapnel, flying concrete
and other debris scything through the air around them. Thus
the defenders waited with trepidation while the vibration of
the approaching aero engines seemed to fill the entire universe.

With a scream the Messerschmitt 110s, normally used as
night fighters, roared at barely treetop height across Ta'Qali,
quadruple 7.92 mm machine-guns and twin 20 mm cannon
from each sowing a sheet of death across the airfield, catching
scurrying figures in their tracks, devastating buildings and
vehicles. A fuel bowser exploded with a monstrous 'whoomf'
which engulfed its unlucky crew as they tried desperately to
steer it out of the aircrafts' path. Jagged shards of glass decapi-
tated two controllers in the Watch Office as they dived for imaginary shelter behind their consoles. Then the aptly-named
'destroyers' were gone, and the dazed and shocked survivors
stared in awe as the Ju 52s rumbled overhead, each disgorging
a trail of floating dandelion seeds, deadly seeds of green and
white and brown swaying in the air from which the birds had
fled.

The defenders at Luqa had precious seconds of warning before the '110s hit them as well, and men flung themselves into
whatever meagre shelter was available. Even so, casualties
were higher because there were simply more people on the airfield, and again there were stunned moments of inertia as the
sinister parachutes blossomed in the sky a bare hundred-yard
sprint above their heads. Then, as at Ta'Qali, every gun in
sight opened up, rifles, Brens and machine-guns echoing the
deeper bark of the artillery. But almost immediately, it
seemed, the deadly airborne flowers were collapsing on the
brick-hard earth and the flames of return fire emerged as the
Fallschirmjäger shed their harnesses. Total confusion reigned

both on the ground and in the air. Two of the trimotor Junkers aircraft collided in a ball of flame and debris, showering pathetic bundles of flesh and blood to terror-stricken graves on the sun-baked earth. Still others, hit by the monstrous barrage from so many guns, exploded or nose-dived. One parachutist desperately hit his quick-release buckle as a stricken aircraft's wing caught his canopy, but he was too close to the ground to deploy his reserve 'chute and splattered on the ground scant feet in front of a young RAF corporal who had barely time to retch in horror before a machine-gun bullet prematurely ended his own life.

At Ta'Qali the men of Ludwig Heilmann's three battalions of FJR 3 were relatively lucky; with no sizeable British Army presence to contend with, their main problems were dug-in machine-gun positions and the 40 mm Bofors anti-aircraft guns whose barrels were rapidly being depressed to deal with ground targets. However, these were mostly arranged around the perimeter and designed to fire upwards and outwards rather than inwards, since it had been largely assumed since Crete that the Germans would not attempt another costly airborne invasion but would land by sea in the vicinity of Valletta – as, indeed, Kesselring's original plan, intercepted by the Bletchley 'wizards', did envisage. For this reason, coupled with the surprise of the assault and the low dropping altitude, the *Fallschirmjäger* suffered relatively light casualties in the initial phase of the operation, although many aircraft were lost, especially as they banked to begin climbing away once they had dropped their loads. This, however, did not really profit the defenders.

The situation was similar at Luqa although casualties there were higher amongst the Germans because the defenders had had those precious few seconds of extra warning, and because of the presence of the Hampshire Regiment. However, the paras outnumbered the defenders by around five to one, and both were essentially infantry units, with no heavy calibre weapons or armoured vehicles except, on the British side, for a few of the ubiquitous Bren Carriers. These, being open-topped, designed for reconnaissance and with armour incapable of withstanding heavy machine-gun fire at short ranges, were next to useless.

At both airfields the paras raced for key objectives: the Watch Offices (or, as the Germans called them, control towers) and the fuel and ammunition dumps which had to be secured, and the AA gun positions, which had to be neutralised if the following wave of gliders was to be able to land in relative safety. (On Crete, the gliders had gone in first, and in retrospect General Student and others had decided this was a mistake.) The fighting at Ta'Qali was brief, almost perfunctory. The crews of a few anti-aircraft batteries fought bravely as individuals for a few minutes, but once the Germans had their light trench mortars zeroed in these pockets of resistance were rapidly eliminated. Moreover, the crews of the heavy guns could not depress their barrels low enough to make them effective against ground targets at such close ranges, even if they had had impact instead of altitude proximity fuzes. Apart from mopping up, Ta'Qali was secured within twenty ferocious minutes.

In the Grand Harbour, meanwhile, the four warships were casting off in order to gain the open sea where their ability to manoeuvre would help them avoid the rain of bombs – but now, in from the sea to the west, came the dreaded Stuka dive bombers, four full squadrons strong. As the warships approached the mole at the harbour entrance the gull-winged aircraft peeled off one by one and commenced their screaming, near-vertical dives. The anti-aircraft gunners on the ships turned their attention to this new and deadly menace. Stukas were normally fairly easy targets, because once committed to their dive they could not manoeuvre, but this time there were so many of them that *some* were bound to get through. Two succumbed almost immediately, though, exploding and showering the sea with debris, but then one scored a hit adjacent to *Penelope*'s 'B' turret which started a fire. Next it was the turn of *Lively*: a bomb scored a direct hit on the stern and the depth charges went up in sympathetic detonation. Her whole stern blown off, she began to settle rapidly in the water and Commander Hussey had no option other than to order 'abandon ship'. The aircraft which had struck her was itself hit by flying metal from the huge explosion and plunged into the harbour fifty feet astern of the stricken vessel. By this time the whole of Valletta and Grand Harbour were wreathed in smoke and dust from the exploding bombs and the continuous AA fire, and the pale blue of what would otherwise have been a beautiful beginning to a morning was grey with death and destruction.

As the second squadron peeled off to attack, the numerous dockside workers who had emerged cautiously from their shelters to observe the spectacle (as they always did) saw that the Stukas' target was *Aurora*; for a moment it seemed as though she would reach the open sea unscathed as the first four projectiles went wide, throwing up fountains of dirty grey-brown water either side of her. Then a fifth bomb hit her bridge superstructure and a sixth so close to her stern that the concussion of its explosion warped the starboard shaft. The ship immediately slewed to starboard, her speed falling away. Only *Lance* escaped being hit and at flank speed weaved and dodged the falling curtain of death as the third Stuka squadron attacked. All their bombs missed but the ship's violent manoeuvring threw off her own gunners' aim and not a single aircraft was shot down.

The fourth wave of bombers returned attention to *Penelope*. 'B' turret was burning fiercely by this time but the firefighters were so far managing to keep the flames away from the magazine, the rest of the guns kept firing and the ship was fully manoeuvrable as she followed *Lance* past the mole. In came the Stukas again as Captain Nichol twisted and turned his ship in desperate avoiding action. It was no use: after several near misses, a second bomb struck the cruiser just above the waterline at the bow, causing her to falter in the water. Three more Stukas had been shot down but they had immobilised the ship, whose Captain could do nothing other than order 'full astern' to prevent more water pouring in through the bow while he returned to the wharf. Harbour fireboats added the weight of their hoses to the ship's own as she backed towards her berth, and the fire in 'B' turret was mercifully soon under control. However, repairs to both cruisers would take time and in the meanwhile, except for a handful of minesweepers, Malta was denuded of naval defence apart from the gallant *Lance*.

The Royal Navy had, of course, been busy elsewhere. The French battleship *Richelieu* had slipped quietly out of Toulon during the night of the 8th/9th with an escort of two cruisers and seven destroyers. Her absence was first noted by a dawn PRU Spitfire flight and an immediate air-sea search commenced. Force 'H' raised steam and sailed from Gibraltar, preceded by Burrough's cruisers and destroyers, while Sunderland flying boats quartered the Mediterranean along her presumed track. However, the battleship had foxed cleverly by heading south-east for a hundred miles before turning southerly, skirting Corsica and Sardinia, towards Oran, so the first searchers missed her and it was not until early evening on the 9th that the vigilant crew of one flying boat spotted their prey. This suited the skeleton crew on the battleship ideally, for now they could use the cover of darkness to speed back to Toulon – but they had not reckoned upon either the speed of Admiral Somerville's reaction to the discovery of their departure, nor upon the efficiency of British naval radar.

Force 'H' by this time was almost abreast of Algiers, having steamed hard all day, and the Sunderland's report indicated to Somerville that the French capital ship should be within his sights by around midnight. He pressed onward, spreading his capital ships in a line abreast formation to give maximum radar coverage to flanks as well as in front. This paid off for the *Prince of Wales*, newest and proudest battleship in the flotilla, spotted a faint radar trace on the north-eastern horizon just as Somerville, aboard his flagship *Nelson*, was beginning to think his fleet had missed its adversary somehow. But the trace seemed wrong, for it showed the French vessel heading back towards Toulon. Somerville knew that if this was true he could not catch her in a stern chase for the two more elderly battleships were only capable of 23 knots and even *Prince of Wales* of only 28, which meant that *Ark Royal* at just under 31 knots was the fastest vessel he possessed. The *Ark*, though, carried another weapon which *could* catch the *Richelieu*, even in darkness, as they had proven on other occasions: the Fairey Swordfish torpedo bombers of 816 and 825 Squadrons, led by Lt-Commanders T.T.C. Jameson and E. 'Winkle' Esmonde.

A strike was readied immediately of eighteen aircraft which lumbered upwards into the starry night in threes, steering on the compass bearing provided by *Prince of Wales'* radar. Laden with a torpedo, the 'Stringbag' could only achieve a maximum speed of 110 mph so they still had quite a long chase to catch the battleship racing away from them at thirty knots. Fortunately, they did not have a headwind to contend with, but even so they did not come up to the French warship until 11:26 pm.

Approaching from 4,500 feet, they were detected by the escorting destroyers as they began their descent to attack altitude (no more than fifty feet) and ran into a furious barrage of fire as they approached, 816 Squadron from the west and 825 from the east in the classic 'crossfire' manoeuvre which meant, in theory, that whichever direction the battleship turned in order to avoid the torpedoes, she would have to turn her flank towards one or the other.

Although the French and Italian warships had begun zig-zagging the moment the approaching bombers were detected, as expected, the crews of the Swordfish thought it strange that there was no fire from the *Richelieu*. Even so, that from the destroyers was bad enough. Their heavier guns laid down a splash barrage in the path of the approaching aircraft while their lighter 20 and 40 mm weapons created a lethal wall of fire in the air through which it was impossible for the Swordfish to penetrate unscathed. First one, then a second and a third aircraft succumbed to the intense barrage as they bored in towards their target, having commenced their run-in from a distance of some 1,500 yards. As they neared the destroyer screen four more aircraft were blasted from the sky, one of them tragically being that flown by Commander Jameson, but the remainder pushed on with determination. The first 816 Squadron torpedo was dropped from 600 yards, closely followed by two more, and moments later 825 Squadron also commenced launching. Two aircrafts' torpedoes hung up, refusing to release, and they broke off their attack, pursued by angry tracer shells. In all seven torpedoes were dropped, three from the *Richelieu*'s starboard quarter and four from port, but another two aircraft fell in the sea as they tried to escape, still at mast-head height. The *Richelieu* was turning to port in an attempt to present as small as possible a target to the torpedoes now running barely over a fathom beneath the placid sea. One of the escorting destroyers, turning to avoid being ploughed under by the battleship, ran straight into a torpedo instead, which blew a gaping hole just aft of her bow. The other three of 825 Squadron's 'tinfish' either missed or sank, but then there was a massive explosion under the *Richelieu*'s stern. A second of 816 Squadron's torpedoes also hit the ship but failed to explode – a common problem, as the Fleet Air Arm had already learned in previous battles. The last torpedo also missed but sufficient damage had been done: the vessel's starboard shafts were mangled and water began pouring into the engineering space.

As the surviving Swordfish disappeared into the night to find

Ark Royal the French Captain of the *Richelieu* conferred with the German naval Commander who was aboard as an observer and advisor. Although the pumps could cope with the influx of water, the loss of half the ship's propulsion machinery would reduce her speed to no more than fifteen knots, which would mean the capital ships of Force 'H' could catch up with her by dawn. Further sacrifice, they agreed, was useless; their decoy mission had been successful and on Sicily the *Fallschirmjäger* were readying themselves to board their Ju 52s. It was therefore decided to scuttle the ship, her skeleton crew being taken aboard one of the destroyers. The Captain of the destroyer which had been torpedoed decided upon the same course and had his own crew taken aboard two other vessels.

Back on Sicily, Walter Koch and all the other officers and men of the *Luftlande-Sturm-Regiment* had finished checking their gear, making sure that the heavy weapons were securely strapped down in their DFS 230 gliders, talking to their pilots and the crews of the Ju 52 towing aircraft, rechecking maps and smoking too many cigarettes. The amphibious contingent of Ringel's mountain division had already departed Messina, transferred from their troopships to landing barges (originally destined for Operation '*Seelöwe*' or 'Sealion', the invasion of Britain) which themselves had made the long journey from Boulogne via canals and railways to the toe of Italy over the last month. The other *Gebirgsjäger* of the 85th and 100th infantry regiments watched the preparations of Eugen Meindl's crack glider unit with apprehension ... heights did not worry them, but they preferred their feet on the ground, even if anchored to a sheer rock face by a single piton, to entrusting themselves to machinery which could fall out of the air with or without enemy intervention. And they knew that once the Junkers aircraft returned from releasing their loads over Malta and refuelled, it would be their own turn to clamber aboard the ungainly aircraft.

General Kurt Student was not present at Calabria to wish the men well as he had done before Operation '*Merkur*' – he was at Palermo to see off the leading units of the 7th *Flieger* Division instead, which was only fair, Koch mused. He and Walter Gericke, together with Hans Jungwirt, Gericke's own number two, Johann Engelhardt, and a couple of other officers were sharing a last bottle of wine before joining the troops of their

1st and 4th Battalions and entering their gliders, eight men per aircraft plus two pilots. Their target was Luqa; the other two battalions would land at Ta'Qali. Gericke raised a hand suddenly to still the conversation. 'Listen,' he said. Then they could all hear it, vibrating from the north-east: the sound of Junkers Jumo engines from countless Ju 88s grasping for height in the sky. The first wave of bombers was on its way.

As if to reinforce the import of the moment, engines started coughing and choking to life on the airfield around Koch and his friends as the aircraft of KG 606 and '806 began warming up for take-off – target Valletta. Smoke and fumes swirled around the men as they watched the dark, ominous shapes manoeuvre with practised skill for their take-off positions, glass canopies glinting in reflected starlight and exhausts belching fire through their mufflers. Engines were revved while pilots held their aircraft on their brakes and completed final checks then, majestically, one by one the bombers soared into the cool sky. 'Our turn soon,' Jungwirt commented. As he had supposed, back in that incredibly dingy Cretan bar, the last few days had been nothing but work for himself and his opposite numbers in the other battalions, making sure that all the men were ready, fit, and fully-equipped and that those who were in hospital or otherwise absent were accounted for. Sometimes, Jungwirt thought sacrilegiously to himself (although he knew others shared his view), it seems as though the Third Reich is strangling itself in paperwork. Then he had to extinguish his pipe; Koch had tossed back the last of his wine and it was time to embark.

Like all gliders, the DFS 230 (DFS — *Deutsches Forschungs-institut für Segelflug* = German Gliding Research Institute) was of fairly flimsy construction, as shown by the manner of General Süssmann's death earlier in the year. Shortly after he had taken off for Crete, his aircraft was caught in the prop-wash from a Heinkel He 111; its towing cable snapped and the glider's wings disintegrated, plunging all its occupants to their deaths. First test-flown by Hanna Reitsch, Hitler's favourite and Germany's most highly-decorated test pilot, the DFS 230 was a small aircraft with cramped accommodation which took off on a wheeled dolly but landed on a belly skid, the wheels being jettisoned as it left the ground. There were two types, the 230A which was the troop-carrying version, and the

230A-1 which was the transport for the heavy equipment.

General Meindl inspected the men of the *Luftlande-Sturm-Regiment* as they lined up beside their machines under the glittering starlight. He had a word for most of his men, especially the Cretan veterans, but even so stomachs contracted and few could help yawning with tension. Then they boarded their aircraft and the Ju 52 towers revved their engines and began moving forward, tow cables unfolding like snakes behind them. As the cables tautened the gliders began to roll, faster and faster until they rose into the air behind the still land-bound Junkers. Then the Ju 52s themselves unstuck and the third wave of the invasion force was on its way, tier upon tier of aircraft with their silent, ghostly companions floating behind them like dozens of flying fish caught on anglers' lines.

As they crossed the narrow stretch of sea separating Sicily from Malta, some of the paratroopers were aware of the brief, intense moments during which they were engulfed in sunlight while the water below was still shrouded in darkness, but few paid much attention to the spectacle, being more concerned that weapons – already checked a dozen times or more – were in perfect working order, that clips for their MP 40 sub-machine-guns were full, that grenades were primed and ready for instant use, that field dressing packs were secure in their pouches and water bottles full . . . not that anyone could have done much about it if some item *had* been missing. The checking was automatic and therapeutic in that it took their minds off the ordeal to follow. A few desultory attempts to make light talk soon fell by the wayside and the occasional filthy joke produced few laughs, for all the men were too keyed up to think of anything except the task ahead.

Soon, all too soon, the sheer cliffs of the Maltese coastline hoved into view. There was, as yet, no opposition. The British Hurricanes were still embroiled with the Bf 109s and Ju 88s ravaging the other side of the island, and the Messerschmitts were taking care to hotly pursue any fighter which tried to break away to intercept the troop carriers. As the formation carrying Koch's battalion passed Ta'Qali, a few puffs of smoke burst around them as the remaining anti-aircraft guns still in action around the airfield tried their luck, but not a single aircraft was hit. Moments later Luqa was in sight, smoke and flames rising from the dusty ground testifying to the fierce firefight still in progress between the men of FJR 1 and 2, and Westmoreland's Hampshires plus the few Bren Carriers of the Cheshires, detached there from their parent battalion at Vittorosia. Then there was the sudden lurch as the glider pilots released their towing lines and the sound of gunfire and explosions grew louder through the swish of the air as the aircraft dived steeply for the ground. Koch, Gericke and their men braced themselves for the shock of impact.

Koch's glider made an almost perfect landing near the eastern perimeter of the airfield and within seconds he and his men had debouched, racing towards a nearby 3.7-inch anti-aircraft gun position ringed with sandbags. The glider's co-pilot threw open the roof hatch and started laying down covering fire with the aircraft's single MG 15 machine-gun. A solitary British gunner managed to loose off a wild round but then Koch's men were in the enclosure and the gunners' hands went up. Other gliders were not so fortunate. One landed close to the control tower, inside the main defensive perimeter established by the Hampshires, and a grenade turned it into an inferno before its occupants could scramble out. Another, damaged by ground fire, stalled into the side of a hangar. One hit a fissure in the iron-hard earth and ground-looped. Others were riddled with machine-gun fire from which few survivors emerged, but the majority managed to land relatively unscathed. Soon the 7.5 and 10.5 cm lG40 recoilless guns and 8.1 cm sGrW 34 mortars were unloaded from the transport gliders and began blasting the British positions, while light 2.8 and 3.7 cm anti-tank guns commenced a turkey shoot amongst the practically defenceless Bren Carriers.

The Hampshires and Cheshires returned the paratroopers' fire with spirit and determination, but the arrival of Koch's and Gericke's two battalions to reinforce Bräuer's and Sturm's two regiments meant that, despite the casualties they had suffered during the landings, the British were still outnumbered by more than seven to one. The fighting was soon at point-blank range with bayonets and grenades, and Hans Jungwirt's face was sliced open from ear to jaw by a piece of flying shrapnel. Colonel Westmoreland rallied a few dozen men in and around the control tower but everywhere else around the airfield the Hampshires were laying down their arms and squatting on the ground under the eyes of watchful paras. General Meindl ordered a cease-fire and detailed his adjutant, Oberleutnant von Seelen, to raise a white flag. The lieutenant, who had spent three years at Oxford before the war and spoke perfect English, walked across to the control tower. Smartly saluting Colonel Westmoreland, he said that further fighting would only cause uneccessary casualties. 'Ta'Qali is already in our hands,' he said, 'and our Junkers will soon be returning with more men. Your soldiers have achieved all they possibly could. There is no dishonour in surrender today.' Westmoreland eyed the young officer with anguish. Then, slowly, he reversed his revolver and extended it butt first. Seelen accepted it gravely and saluted again. Around them the British soldiers laid down their rifles and placed their hands on their heads, while those still in the control tower filed slowly out, relief quite plainly showing on many of their faces. Luqa was now also firmly in German hands.

The codeword 'Prometheus' was radioed back to Sicily, where General Student was already watching the returning Ju 52s and '88s land, many of them showing obvious signs of the intense flak they had encountered, and within an hour the men of the 85th and 100th *Gebirgsjäger* Regiments were boarding their troop transports.

Meanwhile, there had been another drama at sea. At an observation post overlooking St Paul's Bay a terrified sergeant of the King's Own Malta Regiment, awoken earlier by the waves of aircraft passing overhead, stared at what seemed an enormous armada of ships approaching from out of the rising sun. St Paul's Bay was virtually undefended apart from four 25 pdr field guns of the Royal Malta Artillery and a handful of machine-guns. He telephoned his electrifying news to his headquarters in Valletta, whence it was rushed to General Dobbie. The Governor's predicament was acute. Hal Far was devastated by the bombing and its main runway blocked by two Wellingtons which had collided while trying to return, so all the other aircraft which would normally have had three airfields to land on would have to take their chances landing on the perimeter track and in between the bomb craters. The thirty or so surviving Hurricanes were already being refuelled and rearmed, but they alone could accomplish little with only machine-guns against a naval task force; besides, the German fighters and bombers would soon be back. Dobbie ordered Air Vice-Marshal Lloyd to arm his eight serviceable Swordfish with torpedoes while they were being refuelled, knowing in his heart it was a futile gesture but having to make it anyway. The three-man crews of the antiquated biplanes also knew their mission was a forlorn hope, but gamely agreed to give it their best anyway. Dobbie's only other weapon was his last remaining warship, the destroyer *Lance*. He immediately got on the radio and spoke to Lt-Commander Northcott.

'I can't order you to sail, Bob,' he said, 'but you're all we've got.'

'Righto, Sir. We'll head there immediately,' came the irrepressible reply. Like the crews of the Swordfish, Northcott knew his mission was almost certainly suicidal and probably pointless in the long run, but if he could take one Italian destroyer with him he would be happy.

Even as the two men spoke, the German landing barges were waddling in to St Paul's Bay. The defending 25 pdrs opened up and soon shells were falling amongst them. Half a dozen barges were hit, two of them breaking in half and sinking immediately. Dozens of *Gebirgsjäger* were plunged into the water, only their life jackets preventing them sinking like stones under the weight of their heavy equipment, but the bulk of the barges continued to plough inexorably forward. Now the guns of the eight Italian destroyers and two cruisers joined in, hammering at the Maltese gun positions. To begin with their fire was erratic, and a couple of shells even landed amongst the barges, causing howls of anger and derision from the mountain troops. But then, inevitably, they got the range and one by one the 25 pdrs were silenced. The rest of the Maltese garrison, such as it was, quite understandably fled, and the *Gebirgsjäger* began clambering from their vessels up the rocky shore. Pioneers positioned winches on the steeper parts to help bring the artillery, motor cycles and other heavy equipment ashore under the frightened eyes of the inhabitants of the fishing village of St Paul's itself, and soon the limestone-flagged streets reverberated to the smack of heavy cleated climbing boots. There was no resistance.

Meanwhile, at Ta'Qali and Luqa the paras were herding their prisoners into hangars, medics were tending to the wounded of both sides, while other men laboured to manhandle gliders off the runways to give a clear landing area for the Ju 52s which would soon be arriving with their two regiments of

additional mountain troops. At Quormi Colonel Arthur
Bonham-Carter was in a quandary. His Royal West Kents were
sandwiched between immeasurably stronger forces to the
north, north-west and south-east. He got on the telephone to
Colonel Ivan de la Bere, the brigade commander, for instruc-
tions, and was told to pull back to Valletta itself. The Devons
under Valentine were ordered to Hal Far, there to prepare
what defences they could and help in the work of shifting
wrecked aircraft out of the way of those still serviceable.

The eight Swordfish took off at just before 9 am, by which
time the fighting had lasted three hours, and headed north across the island towards St Paul's Bay, skirting Luqa to the east.
The leading aircraft piloted by Lt-Commander Alan Robinson
flew a battle ensign from a post stepped behind the top wing.
They swooped low in a ragged line across St Paul's, being met
by a hail of small-arms fire which tore holes in their fabric but
did not stop them. The Italian warships a mile off the coast
could not bring their heavy guns into play for fear of hitting the
German troops unloading on the shore, but all their smaller-
calibre weapons opened up almost as one. Robinson's was the
first of the valiant force to be lost, a direct hit on the engine
causing an intense fire which swept back into the open cockpit.
With no power, Robinson side-slipped the stricken aircraft to
get the flames out of his face and achieved an almost impossible
belly landing on the water. Incredibly, although suffering from
varying degrees of burns, he and his two crew survived and
were later picked up by the Italians.

The remaining seven machines droned on, wreathed in
deadly shrapnel. A second aircraft fell out of the sky, mortally
wounded, then a third. A fourth disintegrated in an enormous
explosion, presumably from a chance hit on its torpedo. Four
down, four to go, but now they were within range and from just
a few feet above the waves released their lethal cargoes. The
glinting torpedoes disappeared, only a silvery wake betraying
their presence beneath the waves. The Swordfish turned to
starboard as violently as their airframes would stand in an attempt to escape, but all were hit by the pursuing flak and only
one survived to return to Hal Far, watched from *Lance*'s bridge
with dreadful pain by Northcott and his officers. The destroyer
was steaming with a bone in its teeth at her maximum 36
knots, crews of her four dual four-inch gun turrets and fourteen

anti-aircraft positions closed up for action, as were the men serving her eight 21-inch torpedo tubes. She made a gallant but lonely sight to the crew of the Swordfish, who waved in salute as they coaxed their stricken aircraft home.

The Italian cruisers *Luigi Cadorna* and *Giuseppe Garibaldi*, the former with eight and the latter with ten six-inch guns, considerably outranged *Lance*'s four-inch weapons and commenced firing the moment the British warship broke the horizon. However, Italian naval gunnery was never the best in the world and the little destroyer charged on gamely although from time to time a near miss would seem to engulf her in water. Now, though, the Italian destroyers with their own larger 4.7-inch guns were moving towards her in order to protect their larger cousins (which, being light cruisers, had barely thicker armour protection than destroyers), and soon *Lance*'s own weapons could be brought to bear. A savage duel ensued although still there were no hits by either side. Then Northcott ordered hard a'starboard to bring his torpedo tubes to bear, as well as his two aft gun turrets. 'Torpedoes away!' came the cry as the missiles shot from their projectors, heading directly towards the centre of the Italian flotilla. But now, as they closed the range still further, the weight of Italian fire began to count. 'Y' turret received a direct hit, probably from one of the cruisers' guns for it tore it from its mounting. A second shell hit the superstructure below the bridge, carrying away the radio room. But *Lance* was still firing back, and a flash from the bow of the leading Italian destroyer denoted at least one hit. Not a single torpedo scored a strike, but that was par for the course.

Then, suddenly, it was all over. A monstrous explosion near the bow, in either 'A' or 'B' turret's magazine, lifted *Lance* bodily out of the sea and, as she collapsed back, her speed rapidly falling away, she assumed a heavy list to port. Water was pouring in and Northcott knew she had only moments to live. 'Abandon ship! I say again, all hands abandon ship!' The words every sailor dreads rang throughout the vessel and men scrambled up ladders out of the bowels of the destroyer. It was impossible to launch any of the lifeboats because of the acute list, now thirty degrees, but a few Carley floats were cut loose and thrown into the water which rapidly filled with bobbing heads. Two and a half minutes later *Lance* was gone. The Italians picked up 83 survivors from her complement of 190; Commander Northcott was not among them. His parents later collected his posthumous Victoria Cross from Buckingham Palace.

However, *Lance* had scored one hit, and the Italian destroyer *Ascari* was finished off later the same day while limping back towards Messina by the British submarine *Upholder*, captained by Lt-Commander M.D. Wanklyn. Along with the other submarines of the Malta Striking Force, *Upholder* had been at sea during the night of the 9th/10th patrolling for Italian convoys towards Libya, but had been forced to return early due to engine trouble.

Back on Malta itself, General Dobbie was busily organising the defence of Valletta. Those coastal 6 and 25 pdr guns which were not fitted in permanent casements were moved inland and dug in facing north and west, the direction from which the German attack was sure to come. However, with the Hampshires out of action and the Devons at Hal Far, the only regular troops at his disposal were the three battalions of Royal West Kents, Dorsets and Cheshires (and the latter was not at full strength), plus slightly more than a battalion of the King's Own Malta Regiment. There was the Home Guard as well, but Dobbie knew full well he could not expect them to stand up in a pitched battle against the veteran German *Fallschirmjäger* and *Gebirgsjäger*, two divisions strong. Yet Dobbie was determined Valletta would not fall without a fight.

However, the Germans did not have everything their own way. A mixed force of fifteen Blenheims and Wellingtons was despatched from Hal Far to bomb Luqa at 10:30 am and succeeded in capturing several Ju 52s on the ground, destroying seven of them – but the mountain troops had already disembarked so actual German casualties were minimal. But now Valletta and Hal Far themselves again came under aerial attack from the Ju 87s, '88s and SM.79s which returned for the second strike of the day, having re-armed and refuelled on Sicily. Moreover, this time their escorting Bf 109s could stay over the island to protect them for longer, since once the bombers had performed their task the fighters could land at Ta'Qali, where ample British stocks had been captured.

In London, meanwhile, there was pandemonium. The War Cabinet had been in full emergency session since just after 7 am but there seemed – as at the time of Crete – little which could be accomplished. Force 'H' was hundreds of miles away and, in any case, capital ships could achieve little on their own against the German infantry, except run a grave risk of being sunk by the Luftwaffe if they ventured so close to Sicily. Equally, it would take time – too much time – to assemble and despatch a relief force from either Alexandria or Gibraltar, even if spare troops had been readily available, which they were not. *Now* the inadvisability of leaving Malta so precariously defended came home to roost with a vengeance, and there were several acrimonious exchanges between senior naval and air force officers. In the end the hard decision had to be taken: Malta must be left to stand or fall on her own devices. General Dobbie was so informed. 'Well, Jack,' he said to one of his ADCs, 'we're right out on a limb now.'

General Kurt Student had arrived at Ta'Qali with the third airborne wave and was organising the next phase of the assault. His paras were to attack Valletta from the west while the mountain troops descended from the north. 'Short and sharp,' he told his regimental and battalion commanders. 'Keep up the momentum and don't let them rest for an instant.' Then, using some captured Bren Carriers which had escaped serious damage to tow or carry most of their heavy equipment, the paras moved off. The *Luftlande-Sturm-Regiment* was sandwiched in between FJR 1 and 2, and the 85th *Gebirgsjäger* Regiment was on the extreme left, where it would link with the 100th and FJR 3 heading southeast from Ta'Qali. The other mountain troops struggling down the dusty paths from St Paul's would be allowed to join up before the main assault was launched, for Student knew that although he had numerical superiority, the British would be well dug-in and that the natural obstacles as well as the limestone walls of Valletta would be a huge asset to determined defenders. There was no possibility of a battle of movement, it had to be a straightforward frontal assault – always the most costly type of battle, but in this case unavoidable.

Walter Koch missed Jungwirt's solemn but usually cheerful presence as he led his battalion out across the dusty terrain, which was already assuming the characteristics of a giant, bleached griddle even this early in the morning and late in the year. He was flanked by Yuri Hermann, whose ardour had somewhat diminished after his first taste of action, and by Eddie

Dietrich, who had aged months if not years within hours. 'If they live through this lot, they'll both be OK,' was his unspoken thought.

Around Valletta the troops of the English County regiments were digging in, reinforcing the existing anti-tank ditches, checking and adding to the double-stranded barbed wire obstacles, and laying mines. They were helped in this by many members of the Malta Home Guard, who were not enjoying the task at all. These men had already learned that being a member was far from a 'cushy number', involving as it did interminable drill and weapons' training sessions, even though they received extra rations (mostly of sardines or Spam in tins!). Many of them barefooted, in baggy dark trousers and hats, bare-waisted or wearing once-white shirts, they laboured alongside the 'Tommies' and prayed for deliverance: religion has for centuries been a powerful force on Malta. Within the city black-garbed women were chanting the words which had almost become a Maltese litany: '*Gesu, Guzeppi, Marija; Itfghu l-bombi fil-hamrija*', which colloquially means 'Jesus, Joseph and Mary, let the bombs fall somewhere else'.

The 6 and 25 pdrs were sited carefully amongst the bomb shelters which had already been excavated throughout the gardens and allotments around the city outskirts. Many of Valletta's inhabitants who had endured the bombing now fled into the desolate countryside, finding accommodation with family or friends in isolated villages and farms, while the soldiers occupied their air raid refuges and turned them into command and communication posts or ammunition dumps.

It was difficult to believe at around 11 am that several major engagements had already been fought in such few short hours since the crack of dawn. On one side the sweating soldiers dug, wiped sun-blinded eyes, and cursed; on the other sweating soldiers marched, pushed and pulled at recalcitrant machinery, wiped sun-blinded eyes and cursed in a different language. There were in fact further similarities. Professional pride formed part of it. The sense of being confined in a form of arena with the eyes of the world upon you another. Hunger, thirst and fear formed a third link. Blood would soon form a fourth.

The defenders saw the dust first, from vehicles and trudging soldiers, vague silhouettes floating above pools of distorted air. The attackers had already seen the church spires and fortress-

like blocks of the city's buildings rising in pale ochre and white
against the skyline. There had been greater confrontations in
the past and assuredly there would be again in the future, but
for a moment time stood still on Malta. Then the 25 pdrs opened
up, crews racing from half-dug ditches and abandoning half-
filled sandbags in the urgency of the moment.

Some of the trucks and half-tracks stopped to disgorge their
passengers while others carried on into the inferno, and the
German artillery – lighter but more plentiful than the British
– began to return the fire. Still the wraith-like forms of the infantry advanced, wavering, unreal – and deadly. The British
infantry crouched in the meagre trenches hacked from the un-
yielding earth, checked rifle and machine-gun safety catches . . .
and waited. On both sides men flinched as shells cracked overhead or burst nearby. None noticed until they were overhead
the returning waves of German bombers yet again, nor the
paltry dozen Hurricanes rising in sheer defiance to meet them.
Orange flares soared up from the German lines (the pre-ar-
ranged code of the day) to show the Stukas and strafing Messerschmitt Me 110s where they were. Valletta's anti-aircraft
defences, of course, were still very active, and several aircraft
were shot down, but even so the bombers caused devastating
casualties amongst the Royal West Kents on the right of the
British line in particular, for air raid shelters were fewer here
than along the more southerly portion of the perimeter.

As the stunned and deafened defenders dared to raise their
heads again they saw that the enemy in some places were now
only a couple of hundred yards away, and opened fire with re-
newed vigour. The German figures disappeared as they flat-
tened themselves behind low stone walls or into shallow
depressions in the ground, and now their own machine-guns
opened up, providing covering fire for the assault engineers
crawling forward to cut gaps in the barbed wire entangle-
ments. Lying on their backs, shrouded in concealing dust and
smoke from the bombing and the artillery fire, they used their
long-handled wire cutters with the skill of long practice then
placed markers in the ground to show the following infantry
where the gaps were. A few Bren Carriers roared out to try to
stop them in their task, since the wire was too close to the
perimeter for the artillery to be brought to bear, but these were
given short shrift by the German anti-tank guns firing at a

range of a mere four to five hundred yards. Then the paras and mountain troops were shuffling up to the wire at a hundred points, crawling on their elbows with weapons cradled across their arms.

Through the wire. 'Go! Go! Go!' Koch screamed, jumping to his feet and racing forward the remaining fifty yards towards the British trenches, occupied on his sector by Colonel Grimley's 1st Dorsets. A mob of yelling men surged forward with him, ducking and weaving in the trained infantryman's crouch. Dozens of men fell, hit by accurate rifle and machine-gun fire, but there were casualties in the British lines too from the paras' automatic weapons and the German tide was unstoppable. Within seconds Koch and his men were jumping down into the trenches, firing, stabbing with their bayonets, wielding their carbines like clubs. The Dorsets fought bravely and stubbornly but they were overwhelmed by sheer weight of numbers, and first one, then a stream of men began throwing their weapons down and raising their hands. It was the same story all along the line. The battle for the perimeter had lasted barely half an hour.

Koch was unscathed; young Dietrich had collected a nasty bayonet wound in his thigh as he had jumped into a trench but was otherwise all right. Yuri Hermann was dead, his body stitched with machine-gun fire as he raced into the attack. Bruno Braüer, the regimental commander, had a bullet in his shoulder.

The German infantry began sending their prisoners, dazed with the speed and ferocity of the assault, back towards their rear lines. A few British soldiers had escaped back into the city itself, but not many. It was time, General Student decided, to talk to the Governor. Entrusting overall command to General Meindl in case of an accident, Student had himself driven forward in his Horch car, accompanied by two staff officers; a white flag flew from the bonnet.

He was received at the bottom of the city by a smart Captain of the Dorsets who stood on the running board to direct the driver to the Governor's Residence. There he was met by General Dobbie, Air Marshal Lloyd and a delegation of other senior British officers. Smart salutes were exchanged as Student stepped from his car.

Dobbie knew the game was up. All the garrison's code books,

radios and encyphering machines were already being destroyed, as were many of the vital dockyard installations, parties
of Royal Engineers labouring under the beating sun to place
demolition charges. Breech blocks from the guns were being
thrown into the sea. At Hal Far the Hurricanes were being
burnt while the longer-range Wellingtons and Blenheims
hastily departed for Alexandria, carrying as many men cram-
med into their fuselages as they could.

'General.' He inclined his head gravely as he invited Student
into the building.

Student pointed out that he had some 17,000 men poised
around the city's perimeter. If it came to street fighting the
damage and civilian casualties would be unsupportable but the
eventual outcome would inevitably be the same. Dobbie agreed, and the Scottish Knight Commander of the Bath handed
over his sword in token of surrender. The two men agreed the
wording of a short statement Dobbie would broadcast to the
island's population at 3 pm. *Festung* Malta had indeed fallen,
and ultimately the result of these few hours of bitter fighting
would be virtually unchallenged control of the Mediterranean.

Notes

1 All historical details about Malta and the Mediterranean war are correct up to the starting point of the chapter, September 1941. These include the island's defence forces as of this date: historically, they were substantially reinforced in 1942 when the threat of invasion looked real by the Durham Light Infantry, the Inniskillings, Lancashire and Irish Fusiliers, Manchester Regiment and the Royal East/Essex Kents.

2 Walter Koch is a real character. He was the chosen leader of the assault force at Eben Emael in June 1940 and among those who captured Maleme airfield on Crete in May 1941. Historically, he was later wounded in Tunisia and ultimately murdered by the Gestapo in a rigged car smash because of his outspoken opposition to Hitler's order that all Allied paratroopers and commandos should be shot as spies and saboteurs.

3 *Sonnenstich* = sunstroke.

4 Hans Jungwirt was Koch's actual 2ic. Names of other battalion personnel in the taverna are fictitious. Names of divisional, regimental and battalion commanders given in the later orders of battle for both sides are genuine although several were historically not present in the Mediterranean at this time (they were in Russia).

5 'Hercules' was the genuine codename for the planned invasion of Malta, although in actual history it was scheduled for May 1942 before Hitler cancelled it. The outline of Kesselring's crazy plan for the invasion is true: the final plan, its execution and its outcome are based on a wargames study.

6 All unit designations and names of commanders are correct, as are the warships present, etc. Much of this information has not even been published in regimental histories, let alone 'general' accounts of the siege of Malta, and has come from the curators of various museums.

7 The Baedecker episode is genuine.

8 The three Italian liners named were actual troopships.

9 The *Fliegerkorps X* units listed are those which would have been present on Sicily if some of them historically had not been sent to Russia by this time.

10 Bernhard Ramcke did train the *Folgore* Division.

2
Road to Cairo

'Now,' thought Fritz Bayerlein with satisfaction, 'we can really get moving.'

Bayerlein, one of the most respected of General Erwin Rommel's staff officers, had every reason to be pleased as he watched from the white-painted balcony of his hotel room the tanks of the 7th Panzer Division being offloaded from their transport vessels in Tripoli harbour[1]. The date was 9 November 1941. The last five months had been frustrating for everyone after the early successes which had followed the arrival in North Africa of the 5th Light Division in February, reinforced by the 15th Panzer Division in April. Since those triumphant early days, the desert war had degenerated into a stalemate, apart from sharp little exchanges between roving long range patrols and puffs of Flak in the sky when an enemy reconnaissance aircraft grew too bold.

The first German forces in North Africa, skillfully mixing their infantry anti-tank guns with their tanks to give them a great tactical advantage over their opponents (who segregated them), had driven the British out of Cyrenaica (the eastern half of Libya) and besieged the port of Tobruk, thus reversing in one fell swoop the gains made by the British General Sir Archibald Wavell over the previous couple of months.

'This Auchinleck is going to get one hell of a surprise soon,' Bayerlein commented to Robert Borchardt, a Captain in Sonderverband 288, the special commando formation which had been created for behind the lines operations in Africa and the Middle East. Despite the difference in their ranks – Bayerlein was a Lt-Colonel – the two men shared a kindred spirit and enthusiasm for the 'African adventure'.

Bayerlein was remarking on the rather strange appointment of the British General Sir Clive Auchinleck to replace Wavell after the failure of the latter's Operation 'Battleaxe' in June.

Wavell, then the overall British commander in Egypt, had himself attacked Libya in December the previous year and within fifty days had routed the Italian forces in Cyrenaica, taking some 130,000 prisoners and destroying or capturing 450-odd tanks and nearly double that number of guns. This blow forced Hitler to come to Mussolini's aid, as he shortly had to do again in Greece. But by the end of April Rommel, through sheer audacity and energy, had pushed Wavell's forces back to the Egyptian frontier, destroying or capturing virtually the whole of the 2nd Armoured Division in the process. *His* whirlwind campaign had taken a mere twelve days. There, however, the forward momentum ceased, not least because Hitler ordered it. Both sides had incurred heavy casualties in men and materials, though, and the tanks and half-tracks were suffering particularly from the heat and ever-present sand and dust.

Bayerlein sipped his sweet, gritty black coffee and thought back.

Following a weak probing attack in May, in the middle of June Wavell had launched his 'Battleaxe' counter-offensive designed to relieve the Tobruk garrison. After two days' heavy fighting this had been repulsed, but the battle around Sollum had left both sides exhausted and depleted, especially after their efforts only two months earlier. The newly arrived 8th Panzer Regiment, 15th Panzer Division, for example, lost fifty out of its eighty tanks (most were salvaged after the battle, having merely suffered damage to tracks and transmission, etc.) in a single bloody engagement with the 7th Royal Tank Regiment. Nevertheless, Sollum and Halfaya Pass were again firmly in German hands. Wavell, his victory over the Italians forgotten in the face of two major reverses, was removed from command and sent to India. His replacement, Auchinleck, by supreme irony, was an Indian veteran who knew no more of desert warfare than Wavell did of jungle tactics, even though he was a very able leader*.

---

*Auchinleck had returned to England in 1940 and fought in Norway before his new appointment ion Egypt.

Borchardt, himself somewhat misplaced being an old China hand and former adviser to Chiang Kai-Chek, nodded at Bayerlein. 'They've got nothing to match these new Panzer IIIs,' he said, referring to the factory-fresh Mark Js with long-barrelled 50 mm guns being offloaded from the ships at the wharf.

(The first Panzer IIIs in Africa only had 37 mm guns, then had come a short-barrelled 50 mm weapon, but the new long version was incomparably more effective. Both men knew how strange it was that the British had continued to persist with manufacture of the little 40 mm two-pounder tank and anti-tank gun, which was incapable of firing high explosive rounds, after the weapon's failure in 1940. The German armed forces with the 50 mm weapons, both towed and mounted in tank turrets, considerably outranged these, had better armour penetration and could also fire high explosive against 'nuisances' like enemy machine-gun or mortar positions. The same was true of the 75 mm guns fitted to the Panzer IVs, even though at this time they were only short-barrelled themselves. This had so far given the Afrika Korps, as Rommel's force was unofficially known, a significant edge. Unknown to Bayerlein and Borchardt, however, almost at the moment they were speaking a new British gun was being rushed into service, the 57 mm six-pounder. Even this, though, lacked a high explosive capability.)

The tanks and half-tracks of the 7th Panzer Division, Rommel's old command from the 1940 campaign, would be an enormous asset to the stretched resources of the Afrika Korps. The 7th had already earned the nickname 'Ghost Division' because of its ability to appear suddenly out of nowhere to the confusion of the enemy. Now it, and the newly formed 90th Light Division, which was being partly created from odd units already in Africa plus new consignments from Germany, would, the two men hoped and believed, turn confusion into chaos. Many of the personnel in the latter formation had been specially chosen as former French Foreign légionnaires with experience in desert tactics. Borchardt's own commando unit, SV 288, similarly included a large number of men fluent in various Arabic languages and dialects, for Hitler's ambitions stretched further than just knocking the British out of Egypt and denying them the use of Alexandria and the Suez Canal: he was looking further east, to the oil-rich states of Persia and

Iraq. Bayerlein and Borchardt did not know this, of course, but both were intelligent enough to guess.

The British were well aware of the importance of the oil states, not least because they also provided stepping stones towards both India and Russia. Britain had enjoyed good relations with Iraq for years, had a military presence in the country and an important air base at Habbaniya. However, at the beginning of April a coup had brought a new leader to the Iraqi government, Ali Rashid. After early protestations about friendship towards England, the new Premier launched attacks on Habbaniya and other British outposts. These were subdued by the pro-British Jordanian Arab Legion and Rashid fled into exile where he became a propaganda broadcaster, like the English traitor William Joyce – 'Lord Haw-Haw'. In the meanwhile, though, the Vichy French government of Syria had allowed the Germans and Italians to establish three of their own air bases at Damascus, Palmyra and Rayak. When attacks were launched from these against British positions in Iraq, British, Free French and Jordanian forces invaded Syria, forcing an armistice on 14 July under which the country had fallen under British military jurisdiction.

This left Persia (today known as Iran). Winston Churchill had unsuccessfully tried to persuade Stalin into a joint Anglo-Russian occupation[2], but the Soviet leader still appeared to believe in the strength of his non-aggression pact with Hitler, and told the British coalition leader that Russia would oppose any attempt to establish British military rule here. Churchill, obviously, could not afford to lead the UK into war with Russia, even on a limited scale, but did persuade Stalin to sign a guarantee of neutrality assuring Soviet co-operation in the event of any 'foreign' invasion of Persia. Events might have gone differently had Stalin's foremost spy, a man trusted by the German Abwehr and Gestapo named Richard Sorge, not been detected by the Japanese secret police and arrested in Tokyo before he could communicate news of the German dictator's intentions to the Russian intelligence service, the NKVD[3].

For the minute, therefore, it was stalemate in the Middle East, and stalemate in the Western Desert as well where, since Wavell's failure in June the two sides had settled down into a state which many German soldiers described as *Sitzkrieg* – 'sitting war'. The airborne invasion of Crete in May had not materially affected the Afrika Korps in any significant way, even though large numbers of surviving British Empire troops and aircraft had inevitably ended up in Alexandria whence, after resting, refitting and being rooked by the pimps, prostitutes and crooks in Cairo, they ended up in the desert front line. In particular, these included Maj-General Bernard Freyberg's tough New Zealand Division. Many more, however, had been shipped home before September.

The really electrifying news which had thrilled every man in the Afrika Korps was that of the successful invasion of Malta in that month. This threw a completely new light on the whole African situation. Instead of German and Italian convoys being subject to devastating Allied air and naval attacks from the tiny island, the tables were overturned and Malta now stood as an Axis 'cork' in the middle of the Mediterranean, presenting the same threat to Allied shipping to and from Alexandria as it had earlier presented to Axis convoys between Naples, Messina, Taranto and other Italian ports, and Tripoli. Meanwhile, German, Italian and commandered Greek vessels enjoyed virtual immunity during their runs to Tripolitania, and instead of convoys losing thirty per cent or more of their number to British attacks, the proportion during October had dropped to ten per cent and only two vessels out of the convoy transporting the 7th Panzer Division had been sunk. Moreover, only one of those had held any tanks, so the Division's 25th Panzer Regiment arrived virtually intact.

Bayerlein and Borchardt therefore had justification for their confidence as they watched the new tanks being hoisted by crane onto the quayside. Rommel's planned assault to finally subjugate Tobruk in a fortnight must succeed. That thorn had to be removed from their flank before they could make any further headway. Their confidence might have been slightly dented had they known of Auchinleck's own intentions – but only slightly, because even after this short space of time, everyone trusted Rommel.

The British commander in the Middle East, Auchinleck, or 'The Auk' as he was affectionately known, was under great pressure from Churchill to retrieve something from the African situation – and especially to relieve the 20,000-strong garrison in Tobruk, whose supply situation had been particularly badly hit by the fall of Malta. Auchinleck struck on 18 November,

ten days after the arrival of the 7th Panzer Division and before
its troops had really had time to get acclimatised. Thus began
the battle known as Sidi Rezegh, which has subsequently come
to be seen as one of the major turning points of the war . . . and it
could so easily have been a British victory . . .[4]

The opposing forces in this crucial engagement were as follows. In Panzergruppe Afrika were the 7th, 15th and 21st
Panzer Divisions (the latter being the old 5th Light Division
reinforced by the 104th Panzergrenadier Regiment), the 90th
Light *Afrika* Division and the Italian *Savona* Infantry Division. This was the 'Afrika Korps', whose immediate commander was Lt-General Ludwig Crüwell, Fritz Bayerlein being his
chief of staff. The second part of the Panzergruppe was the XXI
Italian Corps, commanded by General Enea Navarrini, which
comprised the *Bologna, Brescia, Pavia* and *Trento* Infantry
Divisions. These were of varying quality, depending upon
leadership, and had been entrusted (under German supervision) with manning the Tobruk boundary. Finally there was
General Gastone Gambara's XX Italian Corps, comprising the
Ariete and *Trieste* Armoured Divisions, which fell under overall command of the Axis C-in-C North Africa, General Ettore
Bastico, who had replaced the jovial but unfortunate Italo
Gariboldi in July. Luckily, Rommel was not one to listen over-
much to a supposed Italian superior officer in whom he had no
faith.

It might be asked why Hitler only allowed Rommel to be
reinforced by a single new Panzer Division at this crucial stage.
The answer lies in a report submitted to him as long ago as
October 1940 by Maj-General Wilhelm Ritter von Thoma, hero
of the Condor Legion in Spain. He had been sent on a fact-
finding mission to Tripoli shortly after the Italians had begun
their abortive attempt to invade Egypt which had ended in
such ignominy. His report stated that logistic problems would
preclude the deployment of any more than four German divisions in North Africa. At that time, of course, Greece, Crete and
Malta had not been invaded and captured. However, the figure
of 'four' stuck in Hitler's mind despite the substantially altered
logistic situation once Malta in particular was in German
hands.

On the British side, Auchinleck fielded the newly created
Eighth Army under the overall command of General Sir Alan

Cunningham. This comprised two Corps, the XIII under Maj-General Alfred Godwin-Austen and the XXX under Maj-General Willoughby Norrie. The latter was the cutting edge of Cunningham's army and contained the 7th Armoured Division – the 'Desert Rats' – equipped with fast-moving but lightly armoured cruiser tanks armed with two-pounder guns, and the 4th Armoured Brigade, which had received the first of its new American M3 Stuart light tanks in July. The British crews rechristened them 'Honeys' because they were such a delight to operate. The other component of the Corps was the 1st South African Division, entrusted with 'mopping up' and protecting the left flank of the advance.

The Eighth Army's 200-odd Matilda and Valentine infantry tanks – the only British tanks sufficiently heavily armoured to allow them to get close enough to the Germans so that they could use their two-pounder 'pea shooters' effectively – were concentrated in XIII Corps as the 1st Army Tank Brigade. In addition, Godwin-Austen had Freyberg's New Zealand Division and the 4th Indian Division. As a tactical reserve, Cunningham also had the 2nd South African Division and the 29th Indian Infantry Brigade Group. Missing was the 22nd Armoured Brigade which had been almost totally destroyed in a disastrous convoy at the beginning of November when seven out of eight transport vessels were sunk by German and Italian aircraft operating out of Malta[5].

Also missing were most of the fresh troops who had been earmarked to relieve the exhausted and emaciated Australians in Tobruk. After the arrival of the colourful Lt-General Stefan Kopanski's Polish Carpathian Brigade to replace the Australian 18th Infantry Brigade in August, it had been planned to substitute the rest of the force — the Australian 24th Infantry Brigade Group – with the 16th and 23rd Brigades of the British 6th Division, which had now finished their task of bringing Syria under control. Also to have been involved was the 14th Brigade of the same division which had been evacuated from Crete in May and was then kicking its heels in Egypt. The Russian refusal to permit an Anglo-Soviet takeover of Persia meant that at least one of the 16th and 23rd had to be held in reserve, but getting any of these troops into Tobruk – an operation planned to start taking place in late September – was a plan scotched by the fall of Malta. Nevertheless, Auchinleck

and Cunningham expected the Australians and Poles to at
least make a feint breakout so as to pin down their Italian
besiegers and prevent them interfering in the main battle
to the east[6].

Auchinleck had protested the folly of attacking the Afrika
Korps without the full reinforcements he had demanded on 29
July – ironically, only three days following Rommel's own de-
mands to Hitler mentioned earlier. Churchill, however, was
adamant. After the collapse of Malta, it was imperative that
Operation 'Crusader', as it had been codenamed, should take
place as quickly as possible. Only by driving the Germans and
Italians out of the 'Benghazi Bulge' and capturing the vital airfields there could the Eighth Army give the Desert Air Force
the wherewithal to neutralise Axis air and sea supremacy in
the narrows between Malta and the Libyan coast. Moreover,
and here Auchinleck and Cunningham reluctantly had to
agree, the offensive had to be launched before the newly
arrived 7th Panzer Division was fully fit for action. The reasoning was sound, but did not take account of the driving force behind Panzergruppe Afrika, the man who had already dismissed
two officers and had a third court-martialled because they had
not pressed forward aggressively enough – Erwin Rommel
himself.

Then aged fifty (he flew to Rome to celebrate his birthday
with his wife only three days before the Eighth Army's attack),
Rommel was already a hero of two World Wars and was shortly
to be awarded a Field Marshal's baton in addition to the other
tangible acknowledgements of his soldiering skill – the *Pour le
Mérite* from the 1914-18 conflict when he had established a formidable reputation as a daring infantry commander on the
Italian front, and the Knights Cross in recognition of the 7th
Panzer Division's achievements in May 1940. A devoted married man, he was shorter than average but powerfully built and
with a firm handshake. He did not smoke and only drank
rarely. One of his favourite pastimes in the desert was hunting,
and he would enthusiastically take off after the graceful gazel-
les which provided a nice change from goat or tinned meat. His
squarish face with its large nose was remarkably unlined apart
from the crease marks of his rather rare smile, and contained
clear blue-grey eyes which held steady under the most piercing
scrutiny.

As an officer in the inter-war Reichswehr, Rommel had written a handbook on infantry tactics which had brought him to Hitler's attention when he was elected Chancellor in 1933, although he was not regarded highly by the head of the armed forces high command, the OKW, Field Marshal Keitel, or many other senior officers. His lack of respect for rank and habit of being right when traditional theory said he should have been wrong made him as many enemies as they did friends and devoted followers. On one famous occasion, when he had been commander of Hitler's personal bodyguard, Der Führer had instructed him not to allow more than five cars to accompany his own in a motorcade. Inevitably, far more Nazi Party dignitaries than could fit into six cars wanted to take part. Rommel turned them all back by blocking the road with a couple of tanks, and despite all the bigwigs' complaints was later thanked personally by Hitler. It was this sort of independent-mindedness which persuaded the German leader to give Rommel command of a Panzer Division in the first place.

Operation 'Crusader' came as a shock to Rommel, because although the signs of an Allied build-up had been noted, German intelligence was not as good as that of the British, who monitored all coded radio transmissions and sent them straight off to Bletchley Park, where they were promptly deciphered by the 'Ultra' boffins. One mystery[7] is why Auchinleck and Cunningham did not hold up their offensive until the 23rd, the date on which Rommel planned to launch his final assault on Tobruk. The German front line on the Libyan frontier would have been an easier nut to crack had the Panzers been already involved in an action elsewhere. But, of course, if Cunningham had waited, Tobruk might have fallen before he could get there.

As it was, all the main elements of Panzergruppe Afrika were well forward, rested after their five-month respite, and virtually up to full strength. Nor did the fact that the British had roughly a six to five superiority in tanks really affect the situation, because not only were the German vehicles generally superior, but their crews had a better grasp of the tactics needed in a fluid battle of manoeuvre.

Cunningham's game plan was audacious and traditional at the same time. After the failure of Wavell's Operation 'Battleaxe', he knew better than to assault the dug-in German positions at Sollum and in the steep escarpments of Halfaya

Pass directly, especially as these now concealed well dug-in 88
mm guns, which were equally versatile as anti-tank weapons
as in their designed role as anti-aircraft guns. Instead he planned to pin and outflank them around Sidi Omar, knowing that
the strongest Axis defending force was the Italian *Savona* Division. This would be the task of XIII Corps, which was to hold
itself in readiness to exploit the hoped-for success of XXX Corps
which was to strike even further south of the main Axis defences, in a sweeping left hook through the desert beyond Fort
Maddalena then heading north-westward directly for Sidi
Rezegh airfield and the Tobruk perimeter only some ten miles
beyond. Depending upon how the Germans reacted, however,
XIII Corps could, Cunningham thought, achieve a breakthrough itself and link up with the garrison if XXX Corps' own
assault was thwarted.

Surrounding Tobruk at this time were, from west to east, the
Italian *Brescia, Trento, Pavia* and *Bologna* Divisions. The
Ariete Armoured Division was further forward, at Bir el Gubi,
with *Trieste* further back around Bir Hacheim. In between the
Bologna Division on the perimeter and *Savona* at Halfaya Pass
were 90th Light and 15th Panzer Division, right on the coast on
the Via Balbia, and 21st Panzer Division to their south-east on
the Via Capuzzo. The 7th Panzer Division was still moving up,
having reached Gazala on the 17th. The Axis forces were therefore off balance, looking north and north-east instead of south
and south-east, because Rommel had uncharacteristically
ignored the warning signs of an imminent Allied attack. On
paper Cunningham's plan therefore looked as though it stood a
good chance of encircling the main components of the Afrika
Korps using XXX Corps (helped by a sally out of Tobruk) as a
hammer to drive the German armour onto the anvil of XIII
Corps.

As with all the best-laid plans, chance, human error and
other factors would play their part in the battle to follow,
though. So did the weather, for a heavy rainstorm during the
night of the 17th/18th turned dust and sand to mud which was
to severely hamper the British attack. While tanks could still
move, their supply trucks would get bogged down. The weather
was at least impartial. Heinz Schmidt, a young Lieutenant on
Rommel's staff who had just been posted to 15th Panzer after
requesting a combat assignment, recalls that when he surveyed

the division's bivouac area on the morning of the 18th it had 'been transformed into a muddy lake a foot deep'. Many men actually died horribly as the wadis filled with water and the vehicles under which they lay sank into the softened soil.

7th Armoured Division led the attack that dismal grey cloud-heavy dawn, so unlike one's normal conception of the desert. Armoured cars of the 11th Hussars and King's Dragoon Guards roared off first through the gaps which sappers had blown in the frontier wire, their task to screen the advance and report first contact. Up until that moment, strict radio silence was to be observed to prevent alerting the German forces, whose officers were themselves concerned at the absence of their leader. (Rommel had flown on from Rome to Greece and was not expected back until the afternoon, by which time the water-logged airfields should have partially dried out.) The British armoured cars were followed by the cruiser tanks of Brigadier G.O.M. Davy's 7th Armoured Brigade – fast vehicles, but under-armoured and under-gunned. Moreover, many were now elderly and very prone to mechanical breakdown. Then, an hour later, the newer M3 Honeys of Brigadier Alan Gate-house's 4th Armoured Brigade began to roll on their right flank.

There was no contact between the opposing forces that first day, apart from a couple of long range clashes with no observable effects between probing British and German armoured cars. Nevertheless, Eighth Army leaguered for the night well satisfied with progress, having established itself in roughly a fifty-mile arc behind the German lines, its leading elements only thirty miles from Tobruk. Because of the weather, the Desert Air Force and the Luftwaffe were equally grounded, so for the moment both sides were punching in an information vacuum. Meanwhile, on the coast XIII Corps had advanced through the wire and was also poised for an assault on the morrow.

Rommel was unimpressed by the reports of the armoured cars' encounters when he returned – both sides regularly sent out patrols and there seemed no particular significance in these. Some of his staff, particularly the commanders of the 15th and 21st Panzer Divisions, Maj-Generals Walther Neumann-Silkow and Johann von Ravenstein, and the C-in-C of the Afrika Korps, Ludwig Crüwell, were less sanguine. All

their desert-honed instincts were sounding off alarm bells and
the two Panzer Divisions were put on alert. But Rommel was
concentrating upon his planned attack on Tobruk, now only
five days away, and the 'desert fox' remained unaware of the
approaching hounds.

The first encounter came the following day, the 19th, when
armoured cars of the King's Dragoon Guards bumped headlong
into their counterparts from the 21st Panzer Division's 3rd Reconnaissance Abteilung as they moved forward to try and discern British strength and intents. A short, sharp battle left
several cars burning before the Germans retreated in the face
of approaching Honeys. Meanwhile, 7th Armoured Brigade
pushed forward unhindered as far as Sidi Rezegh airfield, only
fifteen miles from Tobruk, catching several aircraft still on the
ground and scattering the weak infantry garrison like flies.
However, there was a price to pay, for by the afternoon many
tanks and armoured cars had far outrun their supply lines and
were out of fuel. Meanwhile, on XXX Corps' left flank, 1st
South African Division had made slower progress but was
nearing the positions occupied by the Italian *Ariete* Armoured
Division, a unit they confidently expected to walk over. They
were in for a surprise.

Fully alerted now, Rommel acted with his usual decisive-
ness. 5th Panzer Regiment under the aggressive Lt-Colonel
Stephan was ordered forward immediately while the rest of
15th and 21st Panzer Divisions began redeploying facing
south. 90th Light was sent post-haste to Bardia to join the
Italian *Savona* Division in their well dug-in positions with 23
of the potent 88 mm guns to meet the advance of XIII Corps.
Simultaneously, General Georg Stumme's 7th Panzer Division
was ordered to move up from Gazala.

The inexperienced crews of 4th Armoured Brigade's Honeys
were littered all over the desert after their wild pursuit of the
German armoured cars, and were consequently totally unpre-
pared when Stephan's 85 Panzer IIIs and 35 Panzer IVs, accompanied by four 88 mm guns, fell upon them in the evening
twilight. The ensuing mêlée had a flavour reminiscent of the
Napoleonic Wars. Brigadier Alan Gatehouse knew the enemy's
50 and 75 mm guns outranged the Honeys' 37 mm weapons, so
the tanks' only chance was to use their speed to get in close. In
true cavalry fashion he ordered a charge – and *charge* the

Honeys did, at 40 mph, straight through the astonished German tanks, firing broadsides at almost point-blank range. Past the enemy line, they then wheeled and roared full-tilt back again. It was magnificent, but was it war? As darkness fell and the two sides disengaged, 23 Honeys had been knocked out or immobilised to only seven of Stephan's Panzers. The British succeeded in repairing or towing away twelve tanks during the night, the Germans four. It had been an inconclusive brawl, and there was obvious apprehension on both sides as to what the morning would bring.

Rommel had two main worries. Was the slow but steady advance of XIII Corps towards and around the defensive lines at Sollum, Fort Capuzzo and Halfaya Pass the main assault and the armoured foray from the south a feint to tempt his own armour away; or was XIII Corps itself trying to lure his Panzers into battle in unsuitable terrain while the British tanks broke through the Italian besiegers to relieve Tobruk? The 4th Indian Division was now digging in to pin the German line between Sidi Omar and the coast, while the New Zealand Division had stolen round the Sidi Omar defences and was heading for Fort Capuzzo. For once Rommel dithered, then committed what many of his staff considered a cardinal sin: he split his forces, sending 21st Panzer east to reinforce 90th Light and *Savona* and 15th Panzer south-west towards Sid Rezegh. Meanwhile, 7th Panzer would move out from Gazala at first light but could only be expected to make slow progress over the still waterlogged ground. As it turned out, Rommel's decision was exactly the right one, a prime example of the exception proving the rule.

The 20th was an inconclusive day. Stephan's Panzer group had another sharp encounter with Gatehouse's Honeys in the morning but broke off to await the arrival of the rest of the 15th Panzer Division; Gatehouse would have liked to pursue, but his tanks were now very low on fuel. 7th Armoured Division dug in on the Sidi Rezegh escarpment, up which any German attack would have to come. The South Africans reached the positions held by *Ariete* but apart from an artillery exchange there was no real battle at this juncture. Cunningham had ordered them merely to pin the Italian armour and prevent it from interfering at Sidi Rezegh. Meanwhile, 7th Panzer Division reached the western perimeter of Tobruk and prepared to hurl itself into the fray the following morning. The New Zealand Division launched an assault on Fort Capuzzo and might have broken the Italian defences but the sight of the tanks of the 21st Panzer Division coming up on their left flank forced them to withdraw to await the arrival of the slow-moving infantry tanks of 1st Army Tank Brigade. The next morning would be decisive, one way or the other, and inside Tobruk itself the half-starved but still determined Australians themselves prepared to sally forth and lend their weight to the encounter.

By morning on the 21st the skies had cleared and a blazing sun rose over the minarets of Cairo. The city's inhabitants knew a crucial battle was imminent and the souks were rife with speculation. A slender young Egyptian army officer looked hopefully westwards as he strode across the parade ground towards the Mess for breakfast. His name was Anwar el-Sadat, and he was one of a large number of nationalist-minded Egyptian officers who saw the Germans as the only hope of freeing the country from the English yoke. When the moment arrived, they had contingency plans prepared to take over Auchinleck's headquarters.

In the Western Desert the thoughts on both sides were not on Cairo but on battle. Dots overhead resolved themselves into Wellington bombers heading for the German airfield at Tmini, and Messerschmitt Bf 109 fighters rose gleaming into the pale sky to meet them. Stuka dive-bombers also rose to do battle and Bofors anti-aircraft guns pounded at them from Sidi Rezegh while the tank and anti-tank gunners readied themselves for the Panzers. (The standard British anti-tank gun was the same two-pounder that equipped the majority of tanks, and was ineffective at much more than 500 yards. To supplement them, therefore, Eighth Army used 25-pounder field guns firing high explosive over open sights. This was not a role for which they had been designed but in concentration they had proved they could be very effective – though not, of course, as effective as the enemy's dual-role 88 mm guns which could fire either armour-piercing or high explosive rounds.)

As Stephan's Panzers led off the attack by 15th Panzer Division, its infantry following in trucks accompanied by anti-tank guns, the crews of the Mark IIIs and IVs tensed unconsciously. Heads were pulled into shoulders as the 'crump' of 25-pounder shells landing close by were heard above the din of the tanks' engines, the rattle of their tracks and the incessant hissing of the radios. 'Load AP!' 'AP loaded.' 'Gunner, traverse right . . . target 3 o'clock, 700 metres . . . fire when ready.' Crash! The breech of the 75 mm gun slammed back and the ejected shell case clanged to the turret floor. The loader was already poised with a new shell. A miss. The gunner felt sweat pouring into his eyes as he peered through the telescope and made a minute adjustment to the elevating wheel. Crash! The British Crusader II reared on its suspension like a startled horse. A hit! Tiny figures scrambled from the turret and scurried for shelter from the German machine-gun fire which harried them. But now a Panzer IV was hit and smoke boiled from its interior. A single figure clawed his way from the turret side hatch, stumbled half a dozen paces then collapsed face-down in the sand.

Still the Panzers advanced. In the dust and confusion it was impossible to tell what exactly was happening. The British cruiser tanks were now advancing – there seemed to be hundreds of them – and the range was closing so that the little two-pounders mounted on the backs of lorries could begin to take effect. But so were the '88s firing from several hundred yards behind the Panzers. A direct hit from one of these was always fatal against the thin armour of the British cruiser tanks, many of them elderly A9s and A10s spotted amongst the newer Crusaders. Entire tank turrets were blown yards through the air. Now the infantry were debussing and advancing behind the tanks as they neared the escarpment, but the intensity of the British artillery and machine-gun fire rapidly made them dive for cover and start digging shallow trenches in the sand. But the Panzers still drove forward and for a moment it seemed as though the British line wavered. But wait. Urgent commands crackled over the radios and the Panzers started falling back. 4th Armoured Brigade's Honeys were moving up fast on the division's western flank. 'Pull back! Regroup!' The German tanks fell back through the screening 88 mm guns, the infantry scurrying for their lorries and half-tracks. Stephan looked at his watch. The engagement had lasted barely forty minutes. It felt like forty hours.

Even as 15th Panzer Division withdrew to take stock of the new situation, the valiant Australians emerged from their fortifications, the infantry spearheaded by the garrison's few surviving tanks and armoured cars – the former Matildas

relatively impervious to the fire of the *Bologna* Division's anti-
tank guns. The idea of the sally was to try to break through the
Italian unit's positions on the western perimeter of Tobruk and
link up with 7th Armoured Brigade, but 15th Panzer's attack
had thwarted this. Still the Australians, accompanied by the
fresher Polish Brigade, pressed forward, bayonets glinting wic-
kedly in the morning light. The Matildas trundled relentlessly
onward, shrugging off hit after hit. Their two-pounder guns
cracked and machine-gun fire hosed the Italian trenches, then
the tanks were among the infantry, many of whom threw down
their weapons in panic. But tanks cannot take prisoners in the
middle of a battle and the centre of the Italian line soon looked
like a slaughterhouse. Still the Australian and Polish infantry
came on and the Italian fire became more and more sporadic
and erratic as first a few then increasing droves broke and
began to run – officers usually first, speeding for safety in their
cars. Within two hours the Tobruk defenders had driven a
wedge neatly through the *Bologna*'s lines. But where was 7th
Armoured Brigade?

7th Armoured had become the biter bit. Spurred on by the
timely arrival of 4th Armoured Brigade, it had incautiously
moved down from the Sidi Rezegh escarpment in hot pursuit of
Stephan's Panzers, which were withdrawing in good order and
keeping up a steady rain of return fire. But now their own
reinforcements arrived, and the British tank commanders
could spot the dust clouds of hundreds of vehicles creaming
across the desert from the northwest. The fresh troops and
tanks of 7th Panzer were about to join the battle.

The British advance halted in confusion, then the cruiser
and Honey tanks began to retire, seeking the relative safety of
the dug-in defences on the escarpment. Little did they know it,
but a further threat was approaching from the south-west,
where the 100-odd tanks of the Italian *Ariete* Division had
taken the inexperienced troops of the two South African
Brigades facing them totally by surprise with a dawn attack.
The South African gunners gaped open-mouthed as the little
Italian tanks they had so despised headed at full speed straight
towards them. Italians don't attack, they run! Sheer astonish-
ment was the last emotion registered by many young South
African soldiers that fateful morning of 21 November. *Ariete*
was the Italian army's best formation in North Africa, and had

rigorously trained under German direction since the ignomonious defeats the army had suffered the previous year. As ever, the average Italian soldier did not lack courage, and while *Bologna* was a low grade infantry formation with low morale after the stagnation of the siege of Tobruk, *Ariete* considered itself an elite and was determined to prove it.

It should not be thought that the South Africans were themselves a walkover, though. Individually, they fought back hard without a thought of defeat, but lacking armour or any decent anti-tank guns they were hard pressed to dent the Italian attack, while their sappers had barely begun the task of laying minefields along their front. Some of the Italian M11/39 and M13/40 tanks succumbed to mines, others to fire from the 25-pounders, but the majority reached the South African lines. Here, they did not check – holding ground is an infantry task, not one for tanks – but pressed straight on. Behind the South African lines, cooks and clerks were petrified to find Italian tanks suddenly in their midst. Men dived for shelter as the Italians blazed in all directions. Then, equally suddenly, they were gone, for General Bastico had responded to Rommel's uncharacteristic request for help and had moved *Trieste* up to take over *Ariete*'s positions, freeing his armour to assist at Sidi Rezegh.

As the 7th Panzer Division advanced to place itself on the 15th's flank and the jubilant Italians of *Ariete* endured the wild, bone-shattering ride towards the airfield and its defenders, leaving a shocked and mesmerised South African division behind them, what was happening in the equally crucial frontier battle? The Indians were effectively out of the action except as a cork in the bottle, but so was the *Savona* Division by the same token; neither could move, so in effect it was a trade-off. The main clash was therefore, inevitably, between 21st Panzer Division, reinforced by elements of 90th Light from Bardia, and the New Zealanders who now had the support of 1st Army Tank Brigade.

The British tanks were more numerous by a ratio of roughly three to two than their German counterparts in this sector, and more heavily armoured. But, as elsewhere, their diminutive guns could inflict little damage other than at very close quarters, while the '88s could pick them off one by one while they were still trundling slowly forward. Even at this juncture

Cunningham – an artilleryman himself – forbade the use of the British 3.7-inch anti-aircraft guns (which were virtually the same in capabilities as the '88s) in the anti-tank role. This is a command decision which has often been questioned by writers seeking the reason for the ultimate British defeat at Sidi Rezegh, as the overall battle has come to be known.

At the time, however, Cunningham's decision was sound. Protection of the vital Desert Air Force airfields against the German Stukas had to take priority, and the anti-aircraft gunners were instructed to save their ammunition for aerial targets unless they were under direct threat of being overrun . . . which had not yet happened. Their sea lanes cut by the German occupation of Malta, the British in Egypt were more than usually reliant upon supplies reaching them by air, for convoys up the Suez Canal from Australia, New Zealand, India or Britain via the Indian Ocean or Cape of Good Hope took an inconsiderate length of time to arrive – and the Germans were already stepping up U-boat activity in the South Atlantic to take advantage of the situation.

On the border, the rival forces greeted the same dawn that arose over Sidi Rezegh with similar mixed feelings of anticipation and anxiety. All the tanks on both sides were fully fuelled and ammunitioned and their crews relatively rested. The motorised infantry of the newly formed 90th Light Division were less fresh but the troops were as experienced and keen to acquit themselves as the New Zealanders were to avenge their defeat on Crete. There would be no quarter asked or given in *this* morning's encounter.

Cunningham's fatal error in issuing orders to Godwin-Austen's XIII Corps was the same as that which had confounded the British on several occasions earlier in the war. In splitting his heavy armour from the cruisers in XXX Corps he had anticipated an armoured battle in the relatively open countryside around Sidi Rezegh in which he would enjoy superior numbers, and an infantry and artillery battle of attrition to take the border fortifications. What he had obviously not counted upon was Rommel's surprise transfer of 21st Panzer Division towards the border nor the speed of 7th Panzer Division's arrival in the central arena. Moreover, as had also happened before, co-ordination between the British tanks and the supporting anti-tank guns was weak, whereas the German

Panzer divisions had specifically trained with the concept of mutual support between all arms a principal consideration. This placed the slow-moving Matildas and Valentines at a considerable disadvantage against the practised veterans of von Ravenstein's 21st Panzers, even though they enjoyed superior numbers. With hindsight, the British infantry tanks would have been better employed at Sidi Rezegh, which the Germans *had* to retake, for there they could have used the lie of the land to force the Panzers to approach within range of their guns, instead of having to go out and seek their enemy.

The British moved first in the border sector, the gunners laying down a ferocious artillery barrage which wreathed Fort Capuzzo in huge clouds of smoke and dust while the infantry awaited the order to move forward, sappers first to clear paths through the numerous minefields which protected the Italian defences. Then, wraithlike, the infantry began advancing while the Italian gunners were temporarily unsighted, and the engines of the Matildas and Valentines were revved as they themselves watched keenly for the first sight of the German armour. They did not have long to wait as, from the north-west, the 5th Panzer Regiment and its accompanying motorised infantry and anti-tank guns headed into the rising sun.

The resulting tank battle was one of the largest of the war to date. While the New Zealanders moved doggedly towards Fort Capuzzo – more a line of deeply dug entrenchments and blockhouses in a rough semi-circle than the popular picture of a 'fort' – the tanks advanced to protect their left flank against von Ravenstein's Panzers. However, they lacked the speed to close quickly with their enemy – a Matilda's or Valentine's flat-out maximum was only 15 mph compared with the 25 mph of a Panzer III or IV – and the German 50 and 88 mm anti-tank guns began taking an almost immediate toll while the Panzers themselves for once held back. Bravely the British tanks rolled onward, leapfrogging each other in a practised fire-and-move fashion designed to give the enemy the most elusive targets and their own gunners the best chance of an accurate shot. Their sole advantages were their armour, up to 78 mm thick which was double that on the Panzer IIIs and IVs; and a slightly higher rate of fire. But the '88s could still knock out a Matilda or Valentine at over 1,000 yards, far beyond the range at which they could fire back. And because of their lack of

speed, they could not use the same tactics as 4th Armoured
Brigade's Honeys had.

The overworked British tanks did their best and ploughed
valiantly forward alongside the New Zealand infantry, who
had begun forming 'hedgehogs' – the equivalent of the
Napoleonic 'square' – for all-round defence. The idea of this was
that if the German Panzers pushed the Matildas back, the
enemy armour would have to penetrate in between dug-in infantry positions at ranges short enough that even anti-tank
rifles could take a toll, let alone the heavier artillery. One as
yet unresolved question was whether infantry without armoured support could hold against a Panzer attack. That they
had not against *Ariete* was a fluke, it was thought, occasioned
by the unprecedented suddenness and speed of the Italian
attack coupled with lack of experience amongst the South
Africans. Whether they could, remained to be proved.

South of Fort Capuzzo, anti-tank rounds cracked, near
misses leaving blistering shockwaves of displaced air.
Machine-guns crackled, the Germans' faster-firing weapons
producing a background of ripping calico to the steadier beat of
the British Besas. High explosive rounds from German 105 and
150 mm field guns was echoed by salvoes from the Allied 25-
pounders which broke tanks' tracks and concussed their crews
even if they left the vehicles' armour plating relatively undented. It became hell and dark confusion, a mêlée of mechanical monsters to which blood and gut-wrenching fear were the
natural outriders.

After half an hour, no-one on either side knew who was winning or losing. The radios crackled with incomprehensible
orders. Squadrons tried to reform and regroup but usually
found fresh targets before they could get themselves oriented
in what they thought might be the right direction. The noise
and stink of sour sweat, hot oil and burnt cordite inside the
tanks became almost more than flesh and blood could bear.
Eyes streaming, gunners peered myopically through the
smoke and dust to try to identify the shadowy and swiftly
changing images which flitted elusively through their tele-
scopic sights. Loaders stoically held fresh rounds ready to slam
instantly into red hot breeches, slipping and sliding on the
brass shell cases beneath their feet. Drivers strained to hear
their commanders' directions while trying to maintain course

and avoid obstacles which could strip a track link.

The commanders themselves were little better off. Some operated 'buttoned up' within the turret cupolas for protection, using just their narrow vision slits or periscopes to discern the battlefield; others took the risk of getting shot by standing upright in their turrets in order to gain a slightly better view of what was going on. The latter was a matter of choice. There was no doctrine, no special cachet to operating in the open, no accusation of cowardice for those who preferred a margin of extra security. Indeed, on many an occasion it was the commander who kept his hatch open who survived a hit on his tank by being thrown clear, the one who operated closed down who died because, weakened by shock and loss of blood, he did not have the energy to escape his blazing armoured coffin. As a rule of thumb, those who opted to take their chances in the open made the more successful tank commanders, but suffered a higher proportion of head wounds. At least when their radios broke down – a common occurrence – they could communicate their intentions by semaphore.

Gradually, a semblance of order began to emerge from the chaos. The British infantry tanks, their numbers reduced by about half, began to fall back on the New Zealanders' positions. But the threat of the entrenched infantry and artillery was too much for von Ravenstein, whose tanks had also taken a heavy pounding and were reduced to 44 in running order. The Panzers retired into the lee of Fort Capuzzo. An exhausted silence settled over the battlefield, strewn for miles with blackened wrecks and pathetic, huddled shapes over which the flies swarmed avidly. Dazed survivors picked their way through the wreckage, while medics and stretcher bearers searched among the dead for the still barely living, the teams of both sides often helping one another. Water bottles passed from hand to hand. Black pillars of smoke marked the funeral pyres of the morning's ambitions.

Rommel received the radioed news of the stalemate with disguised concern. He had hoped 21st Panzer could have achieved more than this. All now rested on whether the combined might of 7th and 15th Panzers could dislodge 7th Armoured Division from Sidi Rezegh and inflict a significant defeat on 4th and 7th Armoured Brigades. Both were now tired and had lost heavily. So had the 15th Panzer Division, of course. But his old division, the 7th, was still fresh and eager; and *Ariete* was also on its way.

Cunningham, too, paused for reflection, for much the same reasons. The planned link-up with the Tobruk garrison had gone seriously awry. Fort Capuzzo still held, preventing XIII Corps from advancing any further. And 7th Armoured was dangerously overstretched. The unprecedented breakout of *Ariete* (news of which had obviously been radioed immediately) had left the South Africans out on a limb with nowhere to go except backwards. Other than ordering a general withdrawal, which was politically impossible, he saw no option other than to hold on to the existing gains, pull the South Africans back in the general direction of Sidi Rezegh, and hope the forces around that bleak airfield in the middle of nowhere could hold on until he could bring up his meagre reserves. Meanwhile, the expectant Australians and Poles waited tensely for either help or a counter-attack to throw them out of the perimeter trenches. Few men had much appetite for food, but hundreds of kettles were brewing on stoves – tin cans filled with sand soaked in petrol which gave a fierce heat with no tell-tale smoke.

In Rommel's command car, a captured British Dorchester armoured lorry nicknamed Mammut ('Mammoth'), he and Crüwell conferred briefly with the two Panzer division generals, Neumann-Silkow and Stumme. The planned attack on Tobruk was obviously off for the moment, he said. They would have to rely upon the Italians to contain the breakout and prevent the Australians inflicting any more damage. 21st Panzer Division had at least halted the advance of XIII Corps, who were unlikely to try again until they were reinforced from Egypt, which would take time. The important thing was to defeat 7th Armoured Division and 4th Armoured Brigade – and not just defeat them, but demolish them as the Panzers had earlier demolished 2nd Armoured Division. Once that had been achieved, the 1st South African Division would be trapped in Axis-held country with its lines of communication and supply back into Egypt severed, and would have no other option than to surrender or starve. This would free 7th and 15th Panzers to turn on XIII Corps, after which the assault on Tobruk could be resumed, giving the Germans and Italians access to a major port through which supplies for a new blitzkrieg could be launched into Egypt. Although there was still some hard fighting ahead, Rommel said, in a matter of days the Eighth Army would have virtually ceased to exist.

Unusually, he gestured for Bayerlein to pour each of the men a glass of wine. 'Gentlemen,' Rommel said, raising his own glass, 'This may be slightly premature, but I give you a toast. Christmas in Cairo!' 'Christmas in Cairo!' they responded, grinning broadly.

Rommel then outlined his plan for the assault on Sidi Rezegh. 15th Panzer, which had now seen two days' fighting and was correspondingly weakened, would provide a pinning force with its artillery. The remaining tanks of 8th Panzer Regiment would deploy out of sight to the east to trap any British tanks which attempted to flee, while 7th Panzer Division would assault the escarpment from the north-west. 'And watch out for green flares,' Rommel reminded his officers. This was the prearranged signal *Ariete* was to give when the division's tanks neared the battlefield.

At Sidi Rezegh itself, Norrie was issuing his own orders. The cruisers of 7th Armoured Brigade were to dig in to hull-down positions facing north and north-west, supported by the infantry, artillery and anti-tank guns. The remnants of Gatehouse's 4th Armoured Brigade would hold themselves to the rear as a mobile reserve in case of a German breakthrough and to guard against the arrival of *Ariete* from the south-west.

The German attack came at 3 o'clock, the artillery of both divisions laying down a furious barrage to which the British responded with vigour from their entrenched positions. Overhead, Hurricanes scrapped with Messerschmitts which were trying to protect the Stukas still pounding the airfield defences. As in the earlier encounters, what looked so neat and tidy on the maps rapidly turned into chaos. Individual columns of tanks passed each other in opposite directions without realising they were on different sides. Company commanders had their tanks shot out from under them, baled out and resumed command from another vehicle, often more than once. Dust caked their faces, blisters their hands. In the little British two-pounder anti-tank gun portees (trucks), the gunners fumed as the German 50 and 88 mm guns took a terrible toll while they were only rarely able to fire back. Lorry after lorry burst into flames. One junior officer, 2nd Lieutenant Ward Gunn of the Royal Horse Artillery, saw all but one of his guns put out of action, and that was on the back of a truck itself rapidly being enveloped in flames. Battering out the fire, he manned the gun while Sergeant Grey – the last survivor of its crew – reloaded. Gunn knocked out at least two German tanks before he was killed by a direct hit in the head. For this action, he was awarded a posthumous Victoria Cross. Grey was wounded and subsequently taken prisoner, but survived.[8]

The cruiser tanks were also in difficulty, never before having had to face the long-barrelled 50 mm guns in the new Panzer IIIs which fired with devastating accuracy on a flat trajectory which far outranged their own two-pounders – situation normal, but more so. The British armour had the advantage of prepared positions only so long as the Panzers remained to their front. Once a breakthrough was achieved – and inevitably there was more than one – and the battle became more fluid, they were at a substantial disadvantage. Shortly, the centre of the battle moved on to the airfield itself, conducted amongst a litter of burned-out aircraft and trucks. Norrie was in a quandary. 7th Armoured Division was fighting as hard as it could but its men were tired after their long march from Egypt and the previous day's fighting, the tanks themselves were overmatched, and it was obviously impossible now to relieve the Tobruk garrison. At last count, he had only 28 tanks left. Meanwhile, he kept looking over his shoulder for the dust columns which would herald the arrival of *Ariete* in his rear. Even if the division held the airfield, he realised, it would only be a temporary check to the Afrika Korps. But it is impossible to withdraw in the middle of a tank battle if the enemy has the fuel and reserves to pursue. Something – someone – had to be sacrificed in order that at least part of the division could be salvaged. The agonising decision was taken away from him.

In the dust and turmoil, as we have seen it was often difficult if not impossible to determine friend from foe. Norrie and his staff were therefore unaware that the enemy was so close to the parked cars, trucks and motor cycles of their headquarters until a couple of shells burst in their midst. A pair of Panzer IIIs emerged from the murk over a breast in the ground a mere hundred or so yards away. Frantically, the headquarters staff tried to start their vehicles and flee, but a couple more well-placed shells taught them the inadvisability of this, and helplessly they waited while the tanks, followed by half a

dozen armoured personnel carriers, careened triumphantly up
to them. Inside the command truck the radio officer got a last
desperate message back to Cunningham. 'Norrie captured. 7th
Armoured fighting to last round. We shall . . .' He never completed the sentence as a burst of sub-machine-gun fire shattered his radio. The Lieutenant in the leading Panzer gravely
accepted Norrie's revolver as token of his surrender.[9] Leader-
less, 7th Armoured fought on without direction for the remainder of the day, gradually weakening but still exacting a toll,
while Gatehouse bit his nails and waited for 4th Armoured
Brigade's summons.

As dusk fell and the firing began to die away, the Germans
had recaptured Sidi Rezegh airfield itself and the western edge
of the escarpment. *Ariete* had not arrived as planned for the
simple reason that General Gambara ran out of fuel, a per-
petual hazard in this theatre of operations. The British had no
option but to withdraw, the relief of Tobruk forgotten. It was
'sauve qui peut'. The tattered remnants of 7th Armoured
Brigade, now only with fourteen tanks, led the way east, accompanied by 4th Armoured Brigade and all the division's surviving guns and trucks, the latter with infantry hanging
precariously from every handhold. Evading 8th Panzer Regiment in the darkness, they effected a link-up with the retreating 1st South African Division and refuelled and redistributed
their men and equipment before heading back towards the border wire. Rommel let them go. They were no longer a force to be
reckoned with.

With the failure of the Tobruk relief expedition, the Australians and Poles retired back within their perimeter, leaving the
captured trenches to their original owners. XIII Corps was obviously also forced to pull back under the combined threat of
three Panzer divisions – albeit rather mauled ones. Auchinleck
replaced the unfortunate General Cunningham with Maj-
General Neil Ritchie[10] and ordered Eighth Army back to Mersa
Matruh. Ten days later Tobruk fell and Hitler renamed Panzergruppe Afrika as Panzer Armee Afrika, awarding Rommel
his Field Marshal's baton at the same time. Egypt, the Sphinx
and the Pyramids, Cairo and Alexandria, lay apparently open.

Pandemonium reigned in British General Headquarters
(GHQ), Cairo. After the failure of Operation 'Battleaxe' in the
summer, most of Auchinleck's staff had been convinced that

'Crusader' stood a good chance of success. Instead, within three days Rommel had turned the tables and within a fortnight forced the surrender of Tobruk. Admittedly, his own forces were weakened, but so – drastically – was Eighth Army. Even with the recall of the 6th Division's 16th and 23rd Brigades from Syria to join the 14th Brigade already in the Nile Delta, the British army in Egypt now only numbered this plus the New Zealand and two South African Divisions, 4th Indian Division and the Indian Infantry Brigade Group, and the tattered remnants of the armoured formations which had set out for Cyrenaica with such optimism. These had been re-formed into a 'new' 7th Armoured Division with two weak brigades of cruisers and Honeys and one brigade of Matildas and Valentines. Even with all the heroic efforts of the recovery crews, however, the British could muster no more than ninety tanks. Conversely, Rommel's divisions could now easily be brought back to strength via Tobruk, despite the devastation caused by German and Italian bombing on the harbour and the Australians' own demolition efforts before the gallant garrison finally succumbed. It was as obvious to Auchinleck in Egypt as it was to Churchill in London that the Suez Canal would be Rommel's next objective – but where could he be checked in order to buy time for further reinforcements to arrive?

There was, actually, only one defensible spot, even though it meant abandoning most of western Egypt. Mersa Matruh, it was agreed, was untenable, because it could easily be out-flanked from the south despite its fairly elaborate defences (many built earlier by the Italians) unless there was a strong armoured reserve available. The Americans had promised some of the new M3 Lee medium tanks which had 75 mm guns at least equal to those of the Panzer IV, but given the characteristic speed with which Rommel moved it was uncertain whether they would arrive in time after their long detour around the tip of South Africa. And even when they did, their crews would have to be trained. Maps were therefore scoured, contour lines examined minutely and officers of the Long Range Desert Group questioned intensively about the quality of the ground, whether the sand was soft or hard, whether there were natural obstacles which a defender could use to anchor his positions. In the end there seemed to be only one choice, a sixty-mile strip between the coast and the impassable Qattara

Depression, a huge region of salt flats and quicksands. This meant the position could not be outflanked but would have to be attacked frontally, a role not really suited to Panzers. The railway ran alongside the coast road here and the new defensive line acquired its name from that of a desolate railway station, little more really than a collection of dilapidated huts. Its name was El Alamein, and on 10 December Ritchie was ordered to start amassing all his forces there, to dig minefields and prepare artillery 'killing grounds', lay barbed wire and start thinking earnestly about the disposition of his armour.

The centre of the position was distinguished by a long east-west rock outcrop, the Ruweisat Ridge. Behind this, as a central fall-back point, lay Alam Halfa Ridge. There were other, less significant, points of high ground both north and south, but Ruweisat and Alam Halfa were the keys. The question was, would Rommel attack on the northern, coastal flank to take advantage of the Via Balbia in the event of a breakthrough, or stick by his usual tactic of a southerly hook to try to encircle the defenders? In the end Ritchie made his dispositions as follows. Between the coast and Ruweisat Ridge, where it was ultimately decided an attack was least likely, were the New Zealand and 4th Indian Divisions. South of the ridge he placed the fresh 6th Division and 2nd South African Division flanking 1st South African Division. Behind their centre the Indian Brigade Group occupied the high ground of Alam Nayil and Deir el Munassib. Finally, 7th Armoured Division was placed in reserve at Alam Halfa, ready to strike either north or south once the direction of the main German thrust was recognised.

Meanwhile, Rommel had not been idle. His engineers, assisted by labourers supplied by the Todt Organisation, were slaving to clear the debris from Tobruk harbour, removing sunken obstacles to clear channels for the convoy now concentrating at Taranto. Other engineers sweated to repair as many wrecked tanks and half-tracks as possible, cannibalising sometimes from as many as six vehicles to produce a single 'runner'. Rommel fully realised that speed was of the essence. The longer he left Eighth Army to its own devices, the stronger and better rested it would become and the more difficult would Panzer Armee Afrika's task accordingly be. Field Marshal Albert Kesselring, overall commander for the Mediterranean theatre, concentrated on building up the Luftwaffe to support the

attack, and for the first time the combined German and Italian
air forces in North Africa achieved parity with the Desert Air
Force.

By 20 December Rommel was as ready as he would ever be. A
convoy had arrived on the previous day carrying a hundred
new Panzer IIIs and IVs together with their crews to replace his
losses, and there were also new drafts to fill the gaps in the infantry ranks. There was, equally welcome, plentiful supplies of
fresh meat, fruit and vegetables, and the men of the Afrika
Korps looked forward to a merry Christmas even though it
would not now be in Cairo. On the 21st his troops began moving
up to the border wire, a seemingly endless column of vehicles,
guns and men. There was no resistance as the four- and eight-
wheeled armoured cars of the reconnaissance units fanned out
in a wide arc to screen the advance while Messerschmitts roved
overhead. The leading elements of the army reached Mersa
Matruh late the following day. Although aerial reconnaissance
had revealed no sign of the British, they proceeded cautiously
but their worries were needless. A cheering Egyptian population turned out in force to welcome them, home made German
and Italian flags fluttering cheerfully from numerous windows.
It was like the arrival in Tripoli all over again.

At Mersa Matruh Panzer Armee Afrika paused to allow the
slower-moving infantry to catch up with the motorised formations – the three Panzer Divisions, 90th Light, *Ariete* and
Trieste. The advance continued on the 24th with armoured cars
again in the van to probe the British positions for any weakness
which could be exploited. On Christmas morning 1941 cars
of the 90th Light Division ran into the first minefield at Alamein, bringing down a rain of artillery fire. At this juncture the
British defences were incomplete and consisted of a series of
fortified 'boxes' linked by barbed wire and minefields rather
than a continuous line, because Ritchie's seven divisions and
other odd smaller units could not possibly hope to hold a sixty-
mile front.

The armoured cars withdrew to report back and the Axis
forces leaguered for the remainder of the day, the motorised
units well forward around El Daba, the infantry formations
further back around Mersa Matruh. On both sides the seasonal
festivities were somewhat forced, the laughter a little too loud,
with too much rough Italian and North African wine drunk.

On the 26th, 90th Light made a probing attack in force on the axis of the Via Balbia, where it ran into heavy fire from its old adversary, Freyberg's New Zealand Division. Hampered by the minefields, the advance soon faltered to a halt and the division withdrew under cover of darkness. Rommel himself flew along the line the following morning, seeking a visual impression to add to his reconnaissance and intelligence reports. It was a dangerous if typical adventure. Heavy anti-aircraft fire pursued the diminutive Fieseler Storch and at one point the 'plane was forced down to the deck as Hurricane fighters were spotted. These, however, were chased off by Messerschmitts and the Field Marshal returned safely to his command truck.

Ruweisat Ridge was out, Rommel decided, being too heavily defended by anti-tank guns and artillery. The northern sector was attractive, because a breakthrough here would give instant access to the main coast road to Alexandria, the Royal Navy's principal base in the eastern Mediterranean. The ground was also flatter and more suitable to tanks than that further south. But breaking through was not in itself the most important goal. Destroying Eighth Army in the field was more important than a propaganda victory. Accordingly, Rommel decided to make his main attack in the south, beyond Deir el Munassib, in the sector held by the three brigades of the 6th Division. He redeployed his forces accordingly. 7th and 21st Panzers would spearhead the attack, flanked on their right by *Ariete* and on their left by 90th Light. 15th Panzer would remain in reserve. Meanwhile, the five Italian infantry divisions, which were relatively immobile and possessed few trucks, would dig in on the northern, coastal sector facing the New Zealanders and Indians, pinning them and preventing them from sending reserves to help in the fighting to come in the south. His plans laid, Rommel retired early to his caravan.

The battle of El Alamein commenced on the 27th as 150 tanks of the 7th and 21st Panzer Divisions rolled forward, paths in the forward minefields having been cleared by sappers during the night and marked with flags. Almost immediately, 6th Division's artillery began taking a toll. By mid-morning dozens of tanks and half-tracks had been destroyed or damaged, but the advance had got to within 500 yards of the British positions. Ritchie was in a quandary. Should he commit his armour now, or wait? Even though this was obviously an attack in force rather than the exploratory probe of a couple of days ago, he could still not be certain that it was the main assault. While he hesitated, the Panzergrenadiers were leaping from their armoured half-tracks and wheeling anti-tank guns and mortars into position to add to the fire from the tanks and artillery.

The first breakthrough came just after midday when a company of 21st Panzer's tanks overran a forward anti-tank position manned by gunners of 6th Division. The infantry quickly followed up and the Afrika Korps had a toehold in the Alamein line – but for the moment that was all. It was soon followed by further success, though. Further north 7th Panzer managed to slice through the line between the 1st South African and the 6th Division and immediately wheeled to take 14th Brigade in the rear. Now von Ravenstein put on the pressure and 21st Panzer's tanks advanced with fresh determination at the news of their comrades' achievement. Guns blasted at 6th Division's emplacements, returned by continuing intense artillery fire and heavy, accurate shooting from the two-pounder anti-tank guns. Despite their losses, the Panzers were unstoppable, and followed by Panzergrenadiers who ran behind the tanks which offered a margin of protection from machine-gun fire, by mid-afternoon the two divisions had overrun 14th Brigade and isolated the 16th and 23rd from the rest of Eighth Army. Now Ritchie had no alternative but to throw in his small armoured force and 7th Armoured Division, now commanded by Alan Gatehouse – promoted to Lt-General after his showing at Sidi Rezegh – was ordered forward.

1st South African Division, harried by 90th Light, fell back defensively on the high ground at Deir el Munassib as the Panzer divisions roared through the gap in the line. To their south, *Ariete* continued to probe at the remaining positions of 6th Division, determined not to be denied a share in the glory.

As so often before, the main armoured clash of the day took place in the gathering light of dusk on the plain between Deir el Munassib and Alam Halfa Ridge. The numbers involved were about equal, for both Panzer Divisions had suffered heavily in breaking through the infantry positions, but for once the British had an advantage. Many of the Panzers were almost out of fuel and ammunition after the day's fighting. Georg Stumme and von Ravenstein therefore decided to let the enemy come to them, using the greater range of their own guns to knock off as many of the British tanks before they could bring their own two-pounders to bear. Several cruisers, advancing at speed well in front of the slower Matildas and Valentines, were immediate casualties. Then it became a replay of earlier battles with tanks milling around over miles of desert. But as the heavier British tanks joined the fray, relatively impervious to the German fire, Stumme and von Ravenstein began falling back into the sunset, their numbers reduced to a mere sixty tanks. Gatehouse pursued as long as the light held, then called a halt, his own force also down to a similar number.

Engineers from both sides scoured the battlefield during the night, the superior German half-track recovery vehicles again proving their worth and towing many salvageable vehicles back to safety. Meanwhile, 15th Panzer Division moved forward to take over from the 21st, which had suffered the heaviest losses during the day.

Dawn on the 28th brought no surprises to either side. Neumann-Silkow's fresh division made all the difference and, outnumbered and outgunned, the valiant British tank crews were overwhelmed. To the south, 21st Panzer attacked the remnants of 6th Division from the rear, adding its firepower to that of *Ariete* from the front. Caught in a nutcracker, the two British brigades were forced to surrender. The road to Suez lay open – but the rest of Eighth Army was still intact. Now, after refuelling, the three Panzer divisions swung north, bypassing Ruweisat Ridge to the east and falling on the rear of 4th Indian Division while the *Savona* and *Brescia* Divisions pounded them from the front. Realising the game was up, General Freyberg ordered a retreat, using the coast road to speed his New Zealanders out of the closing trap. The unfortunate Indians fought with all their usual courage and dash, but were in a hopeless position and were also forced to surrender late in the afternoon. This just left the two South African divisions, which fell back on Alam Halfa during the night, determined to buy as much time as possible for the other British troops and civilians in the Nile Delta to effect a second Dunkirk.

In Cairo lights burned all night and the smoke from dozens of bonfires rose into the sky as files were hastily burned. Refugees crowded aboard whatever space they could find on the vessels in Alexandria harbour. Auchinleck telexed the dire news to

Churchill. Within two days Egypt would be lost. Surviving British and Empire troops would withdraw into Palestine, and the Desert Air Force to Habbaniya and the airfields in Syria, but without reinforcements they could not be expected to hold for long.

The convoy of ships carrying a brigade of the new American M3 Lee tanks which was at that moment ploughing up the Persian Gulf towards the Suez Canal turned and started on the long journey back, intending to refuel in Durban and await fresh orders. If they had arrived even a week earlier, they might have checked Rommel's Panzers.

In Cairo, a group of armed Egyptian officers and soldiers broke into GHQ and arrested all the officers there. Auchinleck escaped by the skin of his teeth, having flown to Jerusalem only an hour before, but General Ritchie was captured. Anwar el-Sadat was smiling on the morning of the 30th, New Year's Eve, as the first German tanks and armoured cars roared into the city while muezzins blew from the minarets and jubilant crowds thronged the streets.

Rommel turned to Crüwell. 'Well, we did it.'

Notes

1 7th Panzer Division never actually served in Africa. Historically at this time it was in Russia. However, with the invasion of the Soviet Union postponed to 1942, Hitler could well have been persuaded to grant Rommel his old division so as to help ensure a quick victory over the British.

2 In reality, Britain and Russia were, of course, allies by this time and joint forces had occupied Persia.

3 Sorge was arrested in Tokyo in November 1941.

4 Operation 'Crusader' was in actuality a major British victory which pushed the German forces out of Cyrenaica again and relieved Tobruk, even though Rommel soon bounced back and drove the British back to the Alamein line in 1942.

5 Actually, it was a German convoy which was destroyed at this time by Force K, but Malta was the key to the operation.

6 Historically, the remaining Australians in Tobruk were relieved between 19 September and 25 October, giving Cunningham a much fresher and stronger force with which to hit Rommel in the rear during Operation 'Crusader'. These reinforcements included 32 Tank Brigade.

7 In 'real life' as well as in this narrative.

8 The action in which Lieutenant Ward Gunn actually won the VC under the circumstances described actually took place on 21 November 1941 at Sidi Rezegh but was against the 15th instead of 7th Panzer Division.

9 Such incidents were not uncommon in the desert war. Generals Philip Neame and Richard O'Connor had been captured on 7 April 1941 while driving in a staff car, and Africa Korps CO Ludwig Crüwell on 29 May 1942 when his Fiesler Storch was shot down behind British lines.

10 Historically, as well as in this narrative.

3
Interlude I

Poland in 1939. Denmark and Norway, followed by Holland, Belgium and France in 1940. Greece and Yugoslavia, Crete and Malta, Libya and now Egypt in 1941. Even without mentioning the pre-war take-overs of Austria and the Czech Sudetenland and subsequent smaller territories which had resulted in Bulgaria, Hungary and Romania also becoming German satrapies, Hitler and the Wehrmacht had so far had a good war, and the mood was light in Berlin as the bells rang in New Year's Day, 1942. Jubilant crowds defied the Royal Air Force and sang in the Unter den Linden and Ku'damm while the more sober attended midnight mass in the Kaiser Wilhelm and numerous other churches. Rommel was the hero of the hour.

The mood was more restrained in the Führerbunker buried deep beneath the Reich Chancellery for Hitler forbade alcohol or tobacco in his presence, but the excitement was still palpable. Keitel and Jodl, chiefs of staff and operations of the Wehrmacht respectively, hid their sour feelings beneath bland smiles. Both men detested Rommel and had opposed his every move, denying him time and time again the supplies he so badly needed. Now he had taken the jewel of the Nile without their help. Göring, head of the Luftwaffe, had no personal axe to grind and his plump face was wreathed in genuine satisfaction and amusement. He knew of Keitel's and Jodl's antipathy. But Kesselring's air fleet had kept the RAF's Desert Air Force off Panzer Armee Afrika's back and its Stukas had played no small part in weakening the enemy defences at Sidi Rezegh, Tobruk and El Alamein. After its failure to destroy the Royal Air Force during the summer of 1940 or to blitz London and other English cities into submission subsequently, the air force was back in Hitler's whimsical favour . . . and so, of course, was Göring.

Hitler's own face was animated as he talked, the words spilling out in a furious rush which was sometimes difficult to follow, so fierce was his enthusiasm. His finger darted for emphasis from point to point on the large wall map.

'England cannot hold out long now!' he exclaimed. 'With Egypt secure in our hands their supply lines are too long. Their Mediterranean fleet is doomed. What can they do except skulk in Gibraltar? Our U-boats are decimating their convoys already.'

Admiral Raeder nodded his agreement. The naval C-in-C did not always see eye to eye with his submarine commander, Dönitz, but he was too fair to deny credit where it was due. So far the German High Seas Fleet had accomplished nothing except to lose the *Graf Spee* and *Bismarck*, while Dönitz's U-boats were taking a high toll of Allied shipping in both the North and South Atlantic. From only just over twenty operational boats at the beginning of the year, Dönitz now had over 150. Moreover, in order to nullify the British submarine detection system, asdic, the U-boats had evolved the 'wolf pack' tactic, attacking the vital convoys while surfaced at night instead of launching their torpedoes from periscope depth as previously*. Moreover, the new Focke-Wulf Fw 200 Condor, an aircraft with the range to patrol far out over the North Atlantic from bases in Norway and France, had entered service a few months earlier. This was able to detect and shadow convoys, reporting their positions to any U-boats in the vicinity. And the Royal Navy was unable to provide carrier escorts for any except the most vital and urgent convoys, although the first of a new class of small escort carriers, HMS *Audacity*, had been launched earlier in December.

*Asdic, an acronym for Allied Submarine Detection Investigation Committee, was a device which emitted high-pitched pulses of sound through the water. When they encountered a solid metal object such as a submarine, the sound was bounced back to a receiver on the British warship. The timing and strength of the return signal told the operator the submarine's bearing and range. However, a surfaced submarine, with its shallow draught, could not be detected because the waves on the surface created sufficient 'white noise' to mask its presence. A surfaced U-boat was also a very small target for the primitive radar of 1941 to pick up, and far from all warships were fitted with radar in any case.

After the failure of the Luftwaffe to destroy the RAF in the battle of Britain, Hitler had shelved his planned invasion of Britain, codenamed Operation *Seelöwe* (Sealion), and had concentrated on consolidating and building up the Wehrmacht ready for the planned invasion of Russia. Hitler had always seen the Soviet Union as National Socialism's principal enemy in the long run, and had not wanted to go to war with England in the first place, considering the British natural allies in the fight against international communism. He had originally planned to invade Russia in the spring of 1941, but the trouncing his Italian ally received in North Africa, and then in Greece, had forced two campaigns on him that he did not want. After the invasion of Crete in May, Hitler had wanted to go ahead with the invasion of Russia – codenamed Operation *Barbarossa* – at the end of June, but wiser council had prevailed. One of their considerations was whether deputy Party leader Rudolf Hess may have told the British details of the planned attack when he flew to Scotland on 10 May in an ill-conceived scheme to bring about peace between the two countries. (In fact, he did not, but the high command could not know that.) Thus the army and air force had had six extra months in which to build up their strength, while the capture of Malta and now Egypt had not only secured the Axis powers' southern flank and denied the Royal Navy access to the eastern Mediterranean, but given them a secure base from which to launch further attacks in the Middle East.

Oil was a vital consideration in Hitler's planning. Although gaining Romania as an ally had given Germany access to the output of the Ploesti oilfields, German industry as well as the Wehrmacht required still more. Moreover, an invasion of Persia via Syria and Iraq would give Germany not just control of the Persian oilfields but a door in the south through which to take over Russia's own most important oilfields in Azerbaijan, around the port of Baku on the Caspian Sea.

New technological developments which would assist the Wehrmacht in its invasion of Russia were also on their way. The Afrika Korps' experience in using the 88 mm Flak gun as an anti-tank weapon had put into Hitler's mind an idea for a new heavy tank mounting this gun, and the firms of both Henschel and Porsche had been instructed to build prototypes which were to be ready for a demonstration before Hitler on his birthday, 20 April. In addition, knowing that the main Soviet tanks were armed with powerful 76.2 mm guns, trials were also being conducted into modifications to the Panzer IV to allow it to carry a longer-barrelled 75 mm gun with a higher muzzle velocity, greater range and greater armour-piercing ability.

In the air, plans which had originally been thought of in 1934 for a long-range strategic bomber were also slowly coming to fruition. In 1938 the RLM (German Aviation Ministry) had given the firm of Heinkel a specification for a heavy bomber capable of carrying a 2,000 kg (4,410 lb) bomb load over a radius of 1,600 km (1,000 miles) which would be capable of reaching Moscow from bases in Poland. Designer Siegfried Günter came up with an innovative concept for a sleek machine powered by four 1,000 hp Daimler-Benz engines coupled in tandem. The first aircraft, which received the designation He 177, flew in November 1939 but numerous teething troubles meant that it was not until August 1941 that the first two pre-production machines were sent to a Luftwaffe operational trials unit. The air force test pilots were not satisfied with the aircraft with the result that further modifications had to be made and the first production models did not appear until November.

Another new development was the 'flying bomb', a small unmanned aircraft with a high explosive warhead powered by a pulse jet motor which gave a speed considerably in excess of that which could be attained by a conventional propeller-driven aircraft. So far work on this had been desultory, even though the scientist Paul Schmidt had proven the pulse jet principle as early as 1928 and the Argus company of Berlin had built some motors of this type and fitted them experimentally to Gotha gliders in April 1941. From this work would shortly emerge the V1, codenamed *Kirschkern* (cherry stone).

Even more important were the experiments taking place at Peenemünde, the rocket research establishment on an island in the Baltic run jointly by the RLM and the Army Ordnance Board. Here, trials had been carried out with small liquid-fuelled, gyroscopically stabilised rockets since 1936 under the direction of Colonel Leo Zanssen, Captain (later Major-General) Walter Dornberger and the civilian scientists Wernher von Braun, Walter Riedel, Heinrich Grünow and others. So far these had not produced a militarily feasible design, one with sufficient range and a large enough warhead to justify the expense of manufacture, but the 'boffins' were persistent and it was only a matter of time. Wernher von Braun in particular was determined that the experiments would succeed, because he shared with others a dream that once the war was over a rocket could be developed to put man into space and ultimately on the Moon and planets.

Of even greater potential significance, although at the beginning of 1942 there were few who realised its implications, was the work being conducted by German scientists into controlled nuclear fission. As early as December 1938 Professors Otto Hahn and Fritz Strassmann of the Kaiser Wilhelm Institute of Chemistry in Berlin–Dahlen had written a paper describing the creation of new elements when a neutron hit an atom of uranium. Although it was not appreciated at the time, this was the crucial breakthrough towards the development of an atomic bomb, and the two men's paper became the subject of fervent excitement in Britain and America, to which countries many of the Reich's top scientists had fled after the Nazis' rise to power five years earlier. Hahn and Strassmann had split the atom for the first time and although the experiment had been on a minute scale, it revealed the power which such a transformation of energy could release.

Shortly afterwards, in April 1939, Professor Paul Harteck of Hamburg University wrote to the German War Ministry a letter in which he drew their attention to this development, 'for in our estimation it holds a possibility for the creation of explosives whose effect would be many times greater than those presently in use . . . [The] country that first makes use of it would, in relation to other nations, posses a well-nigh irretrievable advantage.' Five days after the letter arrived, Hitler ordered a total security blackout on anything connected with atomic research. The irony of the whole situation was that the scientists who had most pushed to bring this latest research to the government's attention did so more to avoid being conscripted into the army than for any other reason! Moreover, on the other side of the Atlantic, it took Albert Einstein, one of the German Jews who had fled from National Socialism, until December 1941 to persuade President Roosevelt to inaugurate a military nuclear research programme. This had given Germany a strong head start, which was followed in 1940 by the capture of the Belgian Union Minière's entire uranium stock and the Norwegian heavy water plant at Telemark. At that time Belgium was the only country in Europe possessing uranium ore, having stockpiled some 1,100 tons, and the Telemark plant the only one in the world producing heavy water. At the time of the German invasion of Norway the British, realising the importance of heavy water in slowing down neutrons to the right speed to split the atom, had seized the stock of 26 canisters then in existence and the Royal Navy had ferried them back to England. The plant itself, however, had been left undamaged.

On New Year's Day, 1942, though, Hitler's thoughts were focused on Russia rather than upon new secret weapons. Keitel and Jodl were told to dust off the previous year's plans and modify them in the light of the new situation in the Middle East. Operation *Barbarossa* was to be rescheduled to begin on 1 May.

4
UDI

It was a warm day, but with a strong wind as always near the Cape at this time of year. Pretorious der Vriess, named after the famous Boer Trek leader, adjusted his cap carefully before leaving the small house which he shared with two fellow second-year students from Stellenbosch University, the seat of Afrikaner learning. With his athletic build and short-cut blond hair, der Vriess was a picture of Nordic perfection, especially in the black shirt, riding breeches and boots. It had been some time since he had been able to wear his uniform in public, for the *Ossewa Brandwag*[1] had been outlawed at the beginning of the war, when Smuts defeated Hertzog's stand on neutrality by a mere 80 votes to 67 and took the Union of South Africa into the conflict on the side of England.

Pretorious der Vriess was one of many South Africans, not all by any means of Boer ancestry, who believed that neither the Balfour declaration of 1926 nor the Status of the Union Act of 1934 had gone far enough. While guaranteeing South Africa's independence to determine her own domestic and foreign policies without reference to Whitehall, they still tied the country by oaths of allegiance to the Crown – oaths which, in der Vriess' opinion, would be better offered to Adolf Hitler.

The brotherhood to which he belonged had been formed in 1938 by the fervent nationalist administrator of the Orange Free State, van Rensburg, in direct imitation of the German *Schutsstaffell*, the SS, and its members were united by a solemn oath sealed with their own blood. This ran as follows:

'Before Almighty God, and in the sight of my comrades, I subject myself entirely to the dictates of my people's divinely ordained destiny. I swear to be faithful to the precepts of the

Ossewa Brandwag and to obey the orders of my superiors. On my life I swear a deadly oath of secrecy, that I will cherish and hold sacred the affairs and proceedings of the *Ossewa Brandwag*. I demand that if I should betray my comrades, my oath or my *Volk*, vengeance shall follow me to my traitor's grave. I call upon my comrades to hear my entreaty: If I advance, follow me; if I retreat, shoot me down; if I die, avenge me; so help me Almighty God.'

The language in which the oath was sworn was Afrikaans, the relatively new language which had evolved from the Dutch spoken by the original settlers of the Cape of Good Hope, and all the members of the brotherhood were Afrikaners in whom resentment over British rule and the defeats in the Boer Wars at the turn of the century still lingered like a tumour. Believing in their divine right to rule, and their superiority over the Jews and coloured races in particular, der Vriess and his comrades were all staunch supporters of Hitler and all he had achieved in Germany, in throwing off the yoke of the invidious Treaty of Versailles and restoring German dignity and prosperity. Even the words of their oath were a close reflection of the passage in *Mein Kampf* where Hitler said 'What we must fight for is to safeguard the existence and reproduction of our race and our people, the sustenance of our children and the purity of our blood, the freedom and independence of the Fatherland, so that our people may mature for the fulfilment of the mission allotted it by the creator of the universe'.

Since it was first formed, the *Ossewa Brandwag* had grown to over 40,000 strong, and even though driven underground by Smuts' commission of inquiry, with many of its members – those of German extraction – interned for the duration of the war, it continued to work for South Africa's withdrawal from the conflict. Arming themselves in secret, for the government had confiscated all privately owned firearms, the members of the *Ossewa Brandwag* and other nationalist organisations such as the like-minded *Broederbond*, or Brotherhood, had bided their time and waited for some event to swing public opinion to their own way of thinking. That had now happened.

The rally to which Pretorious der Vriess drove with his fellow students, in the battered old Ford they had purchased between them, that night in January 1942 was to be held in the university grounds, the first public display of their determination since September 1939. The police had been alerted and were expected to be out in force, although no-one really thought there would be trouble for the principal speaker was Dr Daniel Malan, the 68 year-old elder statesman and former Minister of the Interior. He had originally been a supporter of General Barry Hertzog but broke with him in 1934 when Hertzog secured a coalition between the South Africa and Nationalist parties in which Smuts became his deputy. Malan had then formed the Purified Nationalist Party which pushed the policies of national self-determination and apartheid, and had supported Hertzog's eloquent plea for neutrality which had been defeated by Smuts' supporters, forcing Hertzog to resign. Bespectacled and gnome-like in appearance, Dr Malan was a natural orator and this night he had a real subject with which to arouse the passions of his audience.

Hundreds of torches burned, their light spilling back from the trees and giving a pagan flavour to the rally. In one corner of the park a small spotlit platform had been erected and there was a roar of approval as Malan stepped up to the microphone.

He began speaking quietly to the attentive crowd. He spoke of what they all knew, of the proud *Voortrekker* tradition, of the long struggle for independence from British rule, both subjects in which all Afrikaners were well versed. He talked about the hardships of the Great Trek, the way in which Boer lives had paid for English profits in the wars with the Zulus and other tribes. Then he warmed to his real subject.

'Now we see the same happening again. South African lives thrown away to protect an empire which has lost its usefulness ... if, indeed, it ever had one. Two divisions of our finest young men and most experienced officers sailed to Egypt. Tens of thousands of men. Many of you know them, knew them at school, know their sisters.'

There was a ripple of humour at the last sally, but by and large the huge audience was silent.

'The British threw these men away – our comrades, in fact if not always in conviction. They are South Africans, this is their land, their home, the land their fathers have bled and died for in the wars against the English and for the English.

'They were left in the middle of a barren desert to die so that the Generals and their hangers-on would have time to flee a country not theirs in the first place.

'They fought, as soldiers under oath must fight – as you, my friends, will also fight. But most fought against a foe not of their own choosing. Why are England and Germany at war? Adolf Hitler was only protecting his own country's national interests when he acted in self-defence against Poland. He was only protecting his country's security when he attacked France, after giving the Allies months in which to realise their stupidity and make peace. He was only helping a sworn ally when he sent German soldiers to help the Italian forces in the Mediterranean. Adolf Hitler does not want war, never wanted war, only the strength and security in which to rebuild his country.

'Now the British have led us into their war against the man who should be our natural ally, a man speaking a language not that different from our own, a man who wants to impose order and discipline, and a man who is determined to destroy the myth that Jews and gypsies, blacks and coloureds, homosexuals and drunkards, the work-shy and the insane, are as good as the rest of us gathered here tonight.

'Too many good Afrikaner lives were thrown away to further English ambition in the Great War. Some of us fought in our different ways against that madness[2]. Now the same thing is happening again and we must oppose it in every way open to us. General Hertzog is prepared to join us to stop this suicidal folly. He only wanted neutrality, for South African lives to be spared the slaughter of an unnatural war. Now he has seen the true perfidy of Albion. Between us we can overthrow the English lover, Smuts, bring back our young men from their prison camps in Europe, recover our true dignity ourselves, and stop spending our money and resources on fighting England's war.'

There were a few spontaneous 'Heil Hitler's from the black-garbed ranks of the *Ossewa Brandwag* and more muted applause from other sections of the crowd. Malan had spoken the words they all felt but which some still dared not speak. The Jews coined the money from South African gold to fill English coffers. The blacks wanted the vote. Good God, that would be worse than having given it to women. Now South African lives were being thrown away to preserve this empty edifice of an English Empire which no longer even existed except in name.

All of those present had supported either Hertzog or Malan in the crucial vote between neutrality or war in 1939. They had deplored the loss of South African ships (even when owned by English companies) to the U-boats' torpedoes, and the equally vital loss of South African raw materials – chrome, copper, gold, food and others – to fuel Britain's war industries. Now they had a leader, a cause and a bodyguard – the black-shirted stormtroopers of the *Ossewa Brandwag*.

As Malan wound up his speech with an eloquent plea for unity and the crowd began to disperse, some talking angrily amongst themselves, others sunk deep in thought, there was a new mood in the air. A wind of change was sweeping through South Africa, as it would shortly burst over the whole continent.

Two days later, on 7 January, Barry Hertzog rose in the House to make an impassioned plea for South Africa's withdrawal from the war. Smuts, his white goatee beard quivering in agitation, rose to reply amidst cries of 'Shame!' and could hardly make himself heard. The Prime Minister had been as shaken as anyone in South Africa at the army's trouncing at Sidi Rezegh and El Alamein and his own lack of confidence in his earlier policies were apparent to all. Malan called upon the assembly for a new vote on the question of neutrality, and this time the results were reversed. By 91 votes to 56 the South African Parliament elected to sue for peace with Germany.

Then came the vexed question of Simonstown, the naval base which was so vital to Britain's war effort at sea. In 1939, even when pleading for neutrality, Hertzog had argued that the Royal Navy should continue to be able to use its facilities, and there were many now who still felt the same. Without the re-fuelling and replenishing facilities of Simonstown, the Royal Navy would be unable to protect convoys from the Far East, while conversely, would Hitler accept South Africa's withdrawal from the war while his enemies were still granted access? The debate on this issue was far more heated than that on neutrality had been and continued late into the evening, but gradually opinions began polarising and in the end it was decided to close the base to foreign warships of all nationalities except those in distress which would be given three weeks in which to make good their damage. Those still unable to sail after that time, whether British or German, would be impounded.

On 8 January South Africa announced to a stunned world

that she was withdrawing unilaterally from the Commonwealth, suing for peace with Germany and closing
Simonstown. There was shocked disbelief in London and jubilation in Berlin. Another stone had been toppled from the
structure of Empire. How much longer could Britain hold out?

Notes

1 The *Ossewa Brandwag* and all other organisations mentioned in this chapter were genuine. The words themselves mean 'ox wagon picket' and derive from the loosely organised but tightly disciplined groups of men who guarded and protected the wagons during the Great Trek. Smuts, Hertzog, Malan and van Rensburg are historical characters, as are all other background historical details preceding the defeat at El Alamein and its aftermath. Historically, Dr Malan became Prime Minister six years later, in 1948. Pretorious der Vriess is an imaginary name.

2 Malan was editor of the Afrikaner newspaper *Die Burger* from 1915 to 1919 and although he did not join one of De Wet's Commandos in fighting the English during the First World War, was sympathetic and helpful towards their aims.

5
Operation 'Barbarossa'

The first birds had begun singing to greet the dawn just before 4 am on the fine morning of 1 May 1942. A bored Russian sentry checked to make sure he was not being watched by an officer and quickly bent to shield a match with his hands as he lit a cigarette of coarse black tobacco. Then a new sound intruded, a low rumbling on the western horizon which gradually increased to a roar which vibrated the earth. The sentry stared upwards, mouth open in stupefaction, cigarette forgotten, as wave after wave of aircraft thundered overhead. He did not recognise them as Heinkels, Dorniers or Junkers but he did recognise the black crosses beneath their wings and he certainly recognised the tiny black shapes which plumetted from their bellies towards the rows of Polikarpov fighter aircraft parked on the airfield. The first phase of Operation 'Barbarossa', the German invasion of the Soviet Union, was opening with a massive strike to eliminate the Red air force on the ground.

As early as 1940 Hitler had clearly stated his intentions, and Directive No 21 issued from the Führer headquarters on 18 December of that year had read[1]: 'The bulk of the Russian army stationed in Western Russia will be destroyed by daring operations led by deeply penetrating armoured spearheads. Russian forces still capable of giving battle will be prevented from withdrawing into the depths of Russia.

'The enemy will then be energetically pursued and a line will be reached from which the Russian air force can no longer attack German territory. The final objective of the operation is to erect a barrier against Asiatic Russia on the general line Volga-Archangel. The last surviving industrial areas of Russia in the Urals can then, if necessary, be eliminated by the Luftwaffe.'

Hitler had conceived a hatred for Bolshevism and everything it stood for while an infantryman in the trenches of the First World War and had participated in the street fighting which took place in many German cities during 1919 and the early 1920s, along with Göring, Hess, Dietrich, Röhm and others. His hatred of the Soviet regime was as intense as his dislike and contempt for the Slavic races, whom he described as *Untermensch*, or sub-humans. Despite this he was clever enough to realise that the major mistake of the First World War, a conflict on two fronts, was impossible for him to contemplate and that Russia must be held at bay with overtures of friendship while he dealt with France and Britain.

To this end he had signed a non-aggression treaty as well as trade agreements under which the Soviet Union received details of new German technology in return for the raw materials which were needed to put the German economy back on its feet. Then, in 1939 he and Stalin had agreed to carve up Poland between them, and the world witnessed the first *Blitzkrieg** campaign. However, Hitler had seen Russia as Germany's principal enemy from the beginning, and now that his Western flank was secured, the eastern Mediterranean turned into a German-Italian lake, Cairo and Jerusalem were in German hands while only weak British forces remained in Syria and Iraq, and Britain had been reduced to impotence by the defection of South Africa and the depredations of the U-boats on the convoys from the other Dominion countries, his time had come.

The original planning for Operation 'Barbarossa' had envisaged a three-pronged attack with Moscow as the main objective with Leningrad in the north and Rostov in the south as secondary goals. Rommel's success in North Africa and his successor, Generalleutnant Walther Nehring's, in Palestine after Rommel's triumphant return to Germany in the New Year, had caused a reappraisal of objectives. The main thrust was now to be on the southerly flank, aiming to link up with Nehring's Panzer Armee Afrika which would sweep through minimal resistance to Persia and thence swing northwards towards the Caucasus Mountains. There would still be a

*'Lightning war'.

northern and central thrust, though, because Poland and East
Prussia could not be left as an inviting soft core through which
the Red Army might be able to launch a counter-offensive. In
any case, the Baltic port of Leningrad was an equally important objective which was to be tackled jointly by the German
and Finnish armies, the Finns still smarting over the loss of
Karelia to the Russians after the Winter War two years previously. Moscow, although the major communications centre of
the Soviet Union and the hub of all the main road and rail
links, could be isolated by a scissors move in this fashion.
Moreover, the Russians were sure to see it as a major objective
and allocate troops to its defence which would otherwise hinder
the southern drive.[2]

The German divisions assembled in great secrecy for the
onslaught constituted the largest invasion force ever created –
but their adversaries were equally impressive, at least numerically. For the drive on Leningrad Army Group North had been
formed under the overall command of Feldmarschall Ritter
Wilhelm von Leeb, a humourless man who had fought in the
Boxer Rebellion in China and served as a staff officer with the
11th Infantry Division during the First World War. An artilleryman by training, von Leeb had been promoted Generalleutnant in 1929 and received his Field Marshal's baton after
the successful conclusion of the French campaign in 1940. His
forces were the weakest of the three Army Groups and contained only a single Panzergruppe, No V, commanded by
General Erich Höpner. His forces were the 1st and 6th Panzer
Divisions, 36th Motorised and 269th Infantry Divisions, comprising General Georg-Hans Reinhardt's XLI Korps; and the
8th Panzer Division, 3rd Motorised and 290th Infantry Divisions which formed LVI Korps under General Erich von
Manstein. As a reserve they had the 3rd SS Motorised Division
Totenkopf. In support of the armoured spearhead Army Group
North had an additional seven infantry divisions, while it
could also rely on the support of twelve tough Finnish divisions.

In the centre, for the feint thrust on Moscow, Army Group
Centre had been assembled under Feldmarschall Rudolf Gerd
von Rundstedt, probably Germany's leading soldier, who had
fought as a staff officer on the eastern front during World War I,
the front to which he was now returning. Like von Leeb, he was
promoted to Generalleutnant in 1929 and Feldmarschall in

1940, and would have had command of an army group during the invasion of England that autumn had not the Luftwaffe's failure caused it to be called off. The forces under his command also included a single Panzergruppe, No III, under General Ewald von Kleist, with the 11th, 13th, 14th and 18th Panzer Divisions, two motorised and two infantry divisions, plus the elite Waffen-SS Division Leibstandarte *Adolf Hitler*. There were a further 38 infantry divisions in support. The 18th Panzer Division under General Albert Praun was unique in that it was operating Panzer IIIs equipped with schnorkels which would allow them to ford the River Bug which lay in their path. (These vehicles had originally been modified for the planned invasion of England in 1940.)

The southern prong, Army Group South, was the strongest of the three groups because it had the furthest to go, was expected to encounter the toughest opposition, and had the vital task of linking up with Nehring's forces in the Caucasus after taking the vital industrial cities of Rostov and Stalingrad. It was commanded by Feldmarschall Feodor von Bock, like von Leeb and von Rundstedt a scion of an old military family. He shared von Leeb's lack of humour but was fanatically brave, winning the coveted *Pour le Mérite* for leading his troops into battle so courageously during the battles of the Somme and Cambrai in 1917. Like the other two army group leaders, he rose rapidly through the ranks of the interwar Reichswehr but was not promoted Generalleutnant until 1931, although he too received his Field Marshal's baton in 1940. Unknown to Hitler, he was totally opposed to both National Socialism and the invasion of Russia but this did not interfere with his total professionalism as a soldier.

The armoured units under von Bock's overall control were Feldmarschall Erwin Rommel's Panzergruppe I and General Heinz Guderian's Panzergruppe II. Each contained three Panzer divisions – the 2nd, 3rd and 16th and 4th, 5th and 20th respectively – plus one motorised and one infantry division. In immediate support were the 2nd Motorised SS Division *Das Reich* and the newly formed 5th Motorised SS Division *Wiking*, which had been formed during the preceding year from Norwegian, Dutch and Flemish volunteers around the nucleus of one of the parent SS regiments, *Germania*. In support of this already impressive array was an enormous infantry force of 56 divisions, fifteen of them Romanian, two Hungarian and two Italian. The latter were included as a sop to Mussolini's pride and were not expected to contribute a great deal to the offensive . . .

Acting as a mobile reserve ready to reinforce either Army Group Centre or South as need dictated was General Hermann Hoth's Panzergruppe IV, with the 9th and 10th Panzer Divisions and two motorised and two infantry divisions. The last three veteran Panzer divisions – the 12th, 17th and 19th – were held as a general reserve, while the new 22nd, 23rd and 24th Panzer Divisions which had been formed during the winter of 1941-42 remained in France completing their equipping and training. All of the Panzergruppe commanders had distinguished themselves in 1940, von Kleist again in Greece and Rommel of course in North Africa. They were experienced and intelligent soldiers who fully appreciated the magnitude of the task they had been set but had confidence in their own capabilities as well as those of the troops under their command. Unlike Hitler, though, they did not underestimate their foe and the ghastly spectre of Napoleon's defeat in 1812 hung over them like a pall. Moreover, what limited intelligence reports they had received on the most recent Russian tanks to enter service, the KV-1 and T-34, both heavily armoured and armed with 76 mm guns, was a further worry – and as it was to prove, a thoroughly justified one.

Of course, the Germans' own new heavy tank, the Panzer VI, was now going into production. As Hitler had demanded, prototypes of this formidable vehicle with its 88 mm gun had been demonstrated to him on his birthday. Now, after further competitive trials, the Henschel design had been judged marginally superior, but as a sop to Professor Porsche – designer of the Volkswagen, the Peoples' Car – the name he had chosen for his own tank was now given to the Henschel vehicle. It would soon become a name to strike fear into its enemies: Tiger.

The Red Army theoretically outnumbered the German invasion force but was encumbered by a number of factors. Firstly, while the Germans were able to concentrate their divisions into three massive arrows which could penetrate deeply and with great speed, the Soviet divisions were of necessity dispersed in defensive positions all along the enormous frontier. The overall commanders were Marshal Voroshilov in the north,

Timoshenko in the centre and Budenny in the south with a total of 170 divisions in the front line. These included twelve mechanised Corps, six of them in the southern sector under General Mikhail Kirponov, four in the centre under General D.G. Pavlov and two in the north under General F.I. Kuznetsov. Of the three Soviet Generals, only Kirponov was a commander to respect and elsewhere the Russian leadership was pathetically inept. The reason for this lay in the purge of 1937 when Stalin had ordered hundreds of his best officers liquidated, fearing a military coup; these included Marshal Tukachevsky, Russia's leading soldier. Apart from Kirponov, the only leader of real talent to have survived the purge was General Georgi Zhukov, and at the time of the invasion he was in Manchuria.

Quality was also lacking in equipment, communications and morale. Although the new T-34 and KV-1 tanks were available in some numbers, most of the Soviet army's tanks were light vehicles equivalent to the German Panzer Is and IIs, plus BT-5s and -7s which were classed as 'fast' tanks and were the approximate equivalent of British cruisers, being armed with 45 mm guns. One of the main problems the Russians would find in operating their tanks against the experienced Panzer troops, who had so far only seen victory, was lack of communications. Whereas every German tank was fitted with a radio, so units or individual vehicles could rapidly be switched to exploit an advantage, only Russian company commanders had radios, and thus had to communicate with the tanks under their control by means of semaphore using a pair of flags.

Morale was also low. The Tukachevsky purge had reduced the average soldier's confidence in his leaders, who were themselves often totally inexperienced. Political commissars attached to every unit themselves struck fear into the men. There was racial disharmony within the ranks, the fierce Tatars and Ukrainians bearing considerable hatred for the true Russians, who themselves looked down disparagingly on the men from the vassal states; revolution was never far from the surface in the Ukraine, a factor the German army hoped to exploit. In the north, too, Russia had annexed the formerly independent states of Latvia, Lithuania and Estonia in 1940, a fact hardly noticed in the rest of the world because attention was focused on events in France. These peoples, too, could be expected to welcome the Germans as liberators rather than invaders. Finally, the massive Red Army had fought a disastrous campaign against tiny Finland during the winter of 1940-41 which they had only won after suffering enormous losses. If the Finns could hold them to a draw, the average Russian soldier wondered, how could they possibly hold out against the might of the Wehrmacht?

The Red Army had one imponderable factor on its side, and that was the sheer size of the Soviet Union. If its commanders could effect an orderly withdrawal into the hinterland, drawing the Germans ever deeper into a net, with over-extended supply lines, eventually it might be possible to check the advance and then go over to the counter-offensive. However, the Soviet leadership was unready for war and the vast majority of the Russian divisions were unmotorised, so such a scheme was unlikely to be feasible in the face of the fast-moving Panzer divisions.

Little of this was in the mind of Lieutenant Georg Meier during the long night of 30 April/1 May. Having missed the 1940 campaign because of his youth, he had been gratified to have won a commission in a Panzer regiment, which he considered the best wartime consolation prize to being a race driver. His teenage idol had been Ernst von Delius, and he really wanted to drive a sleek 1½-litre BMW, a car manufactured in his home town of Eisenach. But a Panzer III, with its 300 bhp, 11,867 cc V-12 engine was almost an equal challenge. Unfortunately, he found, officers don't drive; they are driven. Thus he found himself easing into the turret cupola in the pre-dawn darkness, having just relieved himself for the third time, with a feeling close to panic which was not soothed by the calm, confident smiles of the other junior officers in his unit, the 3rd Company of 1st Battalion, 35th Panzer Regiment, 4th Panzer Division. Wriggling around on his seat to find the most comfortable position, he plugged in his headset and adjusted the headphones over his black forage cap with its Panzer pink piping. Hans Wischart, the hull machine-gunner who also operated the radio, had already warmed the set up and now Meier checked that the other three members of his crew were ready: Eddie Wolff, the driver, in the left-hand front of the hull; and the gunner and loader, Karl Spaatz and Erich Nolde, who would operate the 50 mm gun, one of the new long-barrelled versions, and the co-axial turret machine-gun. Meier then switched to the company frequency to await orders. Checking his watch, he saw that it was exactly 3.45 am.

Suddenly the darkness was rent with a quiver of brilliant light which seemingly stretched from horizon to horizon, a sur-realistic flicker as though lightning was striking upwards from the ground. This was followed a split second later by an ear-shattering blast of pure white noise as the Korps artillery opened up, laying a withering barrage on the Soviet border positions. Then minutes after it began, the waves of Heinkel He 111s, Dornier Do 217s, Junkers Ju 88s and Ju 87 Stukas began to pass overhead. Reichsmarschall Göring had amassed no fewer than four whole air fleets to support the invasion, a total of 2,770 aircraft, nearly half of them bombers. Then came the order to move out. Switching over to the intercom, Meier ordered 'Driver. Start up!', and the powerful Maybach water-cooled engine burst into a healthy roar of life. The sky was rapidly lightening in front of the Panzers as they began to rumble forward, the trees ahead of them seeming to float above the ground from the white mist which presaged a fine, warm day. The greatest invasion the world had ever seen was underway.

To begin with there was no sign of resistance, although in other sectors of the front it was a different story. Meier spotted the occasional small group of Russian soldiers, border guards bewildered and petrified by the immense and unexpected onslaught. Most scattered and fled, a few raised their arms and were motioned back to be attended to by the following infantry. Here and there the odd man fired forlornly at the advancing tanks with an aging Mosin-Nagant rifle, but the machine-gunners quickly eliminated these foolhardy individualists. The initial surprise soon wore off, however, and the tanks began to fall under fire from prepared enemy artillery posi-tions. When these were encountered, the company comman-ders requested artillery support, which would follow in a few minutes either from the divisional guns or from the sky in the shape of the evil-looking Stukas, sirens mounted in their wheel spats emitting a terrifying shriek as they dived almost verti-cally onto their targets. Of Russian fighter aircraft there was no sign; all the forward Soviet airfields had been practically decimated by the German aerial armada. Onward pressed the Panzers.

The first check came in mid-morning. The battalion's 2nd Company, on Meier's left, had run into trouble in a small village so insignificant it was not even marked on the maps. A heavy KV-1 tank, a monster with armour plate 77 mm thick and mounting a high-velocity 76.2 mm gun, had fired on the Panzer IIIs from cover and succeeded in knocking out four of them with no damage to itself. Meier's Company was asked to provide support by wheeling left and taking the KV in the flank, where its armour was weaker. With the sun over his right shoulder, Meier scanned through his binoculars for the enemy, who was still being engaged frontally by the 2nd Company. Suddenly. 'There it is, Karl! Ten o'clock. Half hidden behind that barn.' Karl Spaatz traversed the turret. 'Steady. Steady. On!', Meier shouted. 'Load AP.' Erich Nolde slammed a round into the breech and tapped Spaatz's shoulder. The gunner searched through the telescope until he spotted the massive bulk of the Russian tank. Its rear hull, and the back of the turret from which projected a machine-gun for local defence against infantry, could just be seen behind the corner of the building. Carefully Spaatz adjusted the range graticule, aiming for the tank's weak spot, the gap betwen hull and turret ring. 'Crash!' The 50 mm gun spat, the breech slammed back and within moments Nolde had rammed another shell into the smoking breech.

The high-velocity projectile hit the Russian tank half way up the turret and screamed off into space, gouging a dent in the armour plate but failing to penetrate. Now other German tanks began to find the mark, and Meier could see the flash of other hits. But the Soviet tank crew now knew they had been outflanked and the KV started reversing, its turret traversing to meet this new threat. Spaatz fired again. And again. The turret was becoming thick with fumes. 'Come on you bastard, die!', Meier thought. And suddenly it did. There was a violent explosion in its rear and the deck plates sailed into the air. Smoke and flames began billowing out of the mortally stricken monster and its crew tried to scramble out, only to be hammered to the ground by a fusilade of machine-gun fire. Meier's Company swung back on to its original course, the thanks of the 2nd Company's commander warming to their ears.

When the KV-1 was examined later, it was found it had received seventeen direct hits before being finished off, a sure indication of problems to come. But Georg Meier and his crew had blooded themselves in their first encounter and for them the war would never again be quite the same.

To begin with the German advance made better progress than anyone had dared anticipate. The Russians had been taken completely by surprise, one of the war's mysteries which has never been properly explained[3]. Up and down the line German communications troops intercepted frantic signals. 'We are being fired on. What shall we do?' Back from head-quarters came the reply, 'You must be mad. And why are you not signalling in code?' Or words to that effect. As expected, the stiffest opposition came in the south, where Georg Meier was operating. General Kirponov was quick to respond to the threat and concentrated his six mechanised Corps in the path of the attack. A sprawling tank battle took place on 4 May between Rommel's and Guderian's Panzers and the Russian tanks, which included the first T-34s seen in this sector of the front.

These were by far the best Russian tanks, being armed with the same 76.2 mm gun as in the KV-1 but with much better mobility thanks to their wide tracks and comparatively low weight (roughly 32 as opposed to 47 tons). Their armour plate was less thick, 'only' 60 mm, but was extremely well sloped to help deflect armour-piercing shot. Their biggest drawback in the early days was that instead of a cupola with vision slits, the commander had a large, flat, forward-hinging hatch. In order to see properly, he thus had to stand upright in the turret, fully exposed to enemy fire; if he closed the hatch he was practically blind compared to German tank commanders. As soon as this defect was realised, urgent modifications were made and within a month new T-34s were coming off the production lines fitted with cupolas.

The clash between Rommel, Guderian and Kirponov took place near Brody, and the Panzer IIIs and IVs suffered heavily at the hands of their more powerfully armed opponents, al-though being able to shoot hell out of the lighter Russian armour. Once again, the divisional 88 mm Flak guns came to the rescue, since only they could penetrate the newer Soviet tanks' frontal armour. Even so, by the end of the first day it was obvious that reinforcements were needed, so Hoth's Panzer-gruppe IV was ordered up in support, its 9th and 10th Panzer Divisions still being fresh. The Luftwaffe was also mobilised in strong support, and the Stukas were able to wreak havoc amongst the massed Soviet tanks as they moved towards their marshalling areas. Moreover, the Russians lacked co-ordination and continued – as the French had done in 1940 – to launch relatively small local attacks which the Panzers were able to contain and defeat piecemeal, rather than concentrating in force. By the third day of the battle many of the Russian tanks were also running low on fuel or ammunition, while mechanical failures caused large numbers to be abandoned. Eventually, after three days' fierce fighting Kirponov was forced to call off the counter-attack and withdraw towards Kiev, the pearl of southern European Russia and a city steeped in history.

Meanwhile, in the centre von Rundstedt's Army Group had encountered far weaker opposition than had been anticipated, except from the fortress city of Brest-Litovsk which proved a tough nut for the infantry to crack and which held out for over a week. Pavlov was a far less able commander than Kirponov and von Kleist's Panzers were able to run rings around his four mechanised Corps which were again committed piecemeal but suffered from even worse co-ordination than the tanks in the south, and five days into the campaign German troops were converging on Minsk and Bialystock. Kleist himself had a narrow escape at one point. While driving up to the forward headquarters of General Gunther Angern's 11th Panzer Division, his car came under fire from a pocket of Russian soldiers who had been bypassed by the Panzers. Kleist's driver was killed instantly and the car swerved off the road into a drainage ditch, Kleist himself being flung clear. Grabbing up an MP 40 sub-machine-gun, he was able to keep the enemy at bay until a couple of SdKfz 251 armoured half-tracks came on the scene a few minutes later to disgorge two sections of tough Leibstandarte *Adolf Hitler* grenadiers. Charging forward with the almost suicidal determination which characterised the Waffen-SS and was often disparaged by Army officers, the SS men made short work of the Russian platoon and gave von Kleist a lift to his destination.

This was only one of several narrow escapes the German Panzer commanders endured due to their propensity for keeping right up close to the front line rather than in comparative safety several miles back, as did most of the senior infantry officers. A couple of days earlier von Manstein had been conferring with other officers in the garden of an intact cottage in a village, most of whose other houses had been set on fire during the fighting to clear them. Suddenly, a Russian BT-7 tank emerged out of the smoke and started pumping 45 mm shells in their general direction. The German officers dived to the ground, one Panzer Major spurting blood from a neck wound, and they might well all have been killed had a well-directed shell from a Panzer IV's 75 mm gun not blown the lightly armoured Soviet tank into mangled scrap iron.

Similarly, a few days later the Russians announced that they had killed Guderian. What had actually happened was that he, like von Kleist, inadvertently drove through a position which was thought to have been cleared of the enemy. However, a Russian rifle regiment had just arrived and its men were disembarking from their trucks as Guderian's driver rounded a corner in the road. Thinking quickly, Guderian ordered his driver to speed up, relying on the dust to conceal the German markings on the car and the unexpected move to confuse the Russians. Audacity paid off and by the time some of the soldiers had woken up to reality and started firing, his car was rapidly speeding out of range!

As the Soviet forces started building up around Bialystock, Hoth's 'fire brigade' Panzergruppe IV was diverted from south to north and, coming around in a sweeping right hook, succeeded in helping von Kleist's Panzergruppe encircle Pavlov's mechanised Corps plus a number of infantry divisions in two major pockets. Although the fighting was fierce, with their retreat cut off and with no supplies getting through, the Russian forces had no eventual choice but to surrender and nearly 300,000 men went into 'the bag'. Stalin had Pavlov himself executed as a traitor and the Panzers continued rattling forward towards Smolensk, beyond which lay the historic battlefield of Borodino, scene of the biggest battle between the French and Russian Grand Armies during Napoleon's invasion of 1812.

In the north von Leeb's Army Group was also doing remarkably well despite the nature of the terrain which was sandy, dotted with lakes and heavily forested, channelling Höpner's Panzers into narrow lines of advance which might have been contained by a more able commander than Kuznetsov. However, the forces in this sector of the front were more evenly matched than elsewhere, two Panzer Korps against two mechanised Corps, and the superiority of German command and communications, coupled with excellent aerial support, again proved themselves. After a fierce battle near Tilsit, Reinhardt broke through, scattering the opposition, while von Manstein raced on towards Dvinsk (Daugavpils) and the important bridges over the River Dvina. Amazingly, these were captured intact because his Panzers arrived on the scene before Russian engineers had completed placing their demolition charges. Although there was heavy fighting in the town itself, Manstein's troops eventually won the day, but by this time they had far outstripped the rest of Army Group North and, in fact, were threatened from the rear by other Soviet forces which they had bypassed and which were now steadily retreating in the face of Reinhardt's Korps and the slower-moving German infantry divisions. (It must not be forgotten that, although the premier formations of the German Army were fully motorised in 1940, even by 1942 industry had proven unable to match demand to supply, so the majority of troops had to march in First World War fashion from railheads to their assembly points, while the artillery and supply wagons were still mostly horse-drawn.)

Reacting himself to orders from Hitler, von Leeb ordered Manstein to consolidate the bridgehead at Dvinsk and wait for reinforcements to reach him, although his own inclination was to push straight on towards Leningrad, through the so-called Stalin Line south of Lake Peipsi then swinging north to the west of Lake Ilmen. The delay was ill advised, because by the time the SS *Totenkopf* Division arrived to lend its support to Manstein's Panzers, the Russians had regrouped substantial forces around Pskov, on the northern flank of the Stalin Line. The capture of the Latvian capital, Riga, on the Baltic coast, was therefore decided to be unimportant. It could be isolated and taken at leisure later; the destruction of the Soviet field army had to take priority.

18th Army, operating on the Panzergruppe's left flank along the coast, had already captured the Lithuanian capital of Lepaya and now pushed across the Dvina into Estonia, heading for Tallinn, while Reinhardt and Manstein, their forces reunited, struck almost directly towards Pskov, Reinhardt frontally to pin the Russians and Manstein in a right hook intended to trap them. To achieve this, Manstein had to break

through the Stalin Line, which was more a chain of fortifications than a continuous structure, as the Maginot Line had
been. Moreover, it had similarly been designed with memories
of the First World War more in mind than the needs of modern,
fluid warfare, and posed little obstacle to tanks except in the
extreme north, for the area around Pskov was thick marsh and
forest through which ran only marginal roads, built of felled
trees laid in the mud. The advance through these was therefore
entrusted to the SS *Totenkopf* Division, while the Panzers
headed south of them to Ostrov.

The Russians did not give up the Stalin Line easily, and
riposted with a vigorous counter-attack which Reinhardt and
Manstein were only able to contain and turn with difficulty, the
8th Panzer Division under General Erich Brandenberger
suffering particularly grievously. By the time the line was
breached and the Panzers rolling again, its 10th Panzer
Regiment had been reduced to a mere 27 tanks and the division
had to be withdrawn from the line, its place taken by the reserve 12th Panzer Division.

Thus reinforced, it was a mere fortnight after the campaign
commenced that German troops reached the River Luga a mere
sixty miles from Leningrad. Pontoon bridges were thrown
across and the Panzers continued to roll, reaching Novgorod on
22 May. With the Finns pushing down from the north, Russian
forces in this region were in grave danger of being trapped, and
although many succeeded in escaping to the south-east, ap-
proximately another quarter of a million Russian soldiers went
into captivity and Leningrad was completely cut off by the end
of the month. (Riga fell on the 22nd after an abortive effort to
evacuate by sea back to Leningrad, which was foiled by the
Luftwaffe.) The citizens of the three Baltic states, Latvia,
Lithuania and Estonia, also responded as predicted, welcoming
the German soldiery with smiles and flowers. Many of their
young men would shortly be welcomed into the ranks of the
Waffen-SS, forming three complete new divisions to fight
against the Russians. (Recruitment of German nationals into
the SS was rigidly controlled by the Army, with the result that,
in order to build up numbers, Himmler had to look for volunteers from those countries overrun by the Army.)

Despite the initial euphoria of liberation from the hated
Moscow rule, however, the cheers amongst the people of the

Baltic states began to subside as the units of *Einsatzgruppen* – murder squads – followed up the front-line troops. These, faithful to Hitler's racial policies, were tasked with the extermination of Jews and other undesirables, for Hitler had declared total war on the Russian peoples and the men and women of the occupied areas could only protest in vain. Hitler's so-called 'Commissar Order' of March 1941, over a year before the actual invasion took place but never rescinded, was perhaps one of his greatest blunders, because it alienated people who would otherwise have fought valiantly for him. What is even more surprising, really, is that so many whose friends and families became victims continued to support the anti-Stalinist 'crusade', by which name the invasion had already become popular. At least part of the answer lies in the fact that the Soviet government treated its vassals, especially the Jews, even more harshly than did the Germans.

Hitler's order provoked serious dissent amongst his field commanders even while it was applauded by the sycophants like Keitel and Jodl on the General Staff and fanatics like Himmler and Goebbels. For the most part, however, the Generals kept their feelings to themselves. They had sworn oaths of fealty and, besides, they had new lands to conquer in order to heap further laurels on their own heads.

The Führer's actual words are worth repeating since they account for much of the savagery which took place on the eastern front, savagery which was alien to men like Rommel, Guderian and Manstein to name but three who believed in fighting a 'clean' war, insofar as war can ever be clean, with determination and aggression but without hatred. He said: 'The war against Russia will be such that it cannot be conducted in a knightly fashion. The struggle is one of ideologies and racial differences and will have to be conducted with unprecedented, unmerciful and unrelenting hardness. All officers will have to rid themselves of obsolete ideologies ... I insist absolutely that my orders be executed without contradiction ... German soldiers guilty of breaking international law ... will be excused. Russia has not participated in the Hague Convention[3] and therefore has no rights under it.'

By the time Leningrad was invested, Georg Meier and the rest of Army Group South had penetrated over 300 miles into Russia, and were similarly greeted in many places by smiles and cheers from Ukrainian villagers. However, Kirponos had been ordered by Stalin to hold Kiev at all costs and another major battle was imminent. Meier now classed himself as a veteran, and was well pleased with his crew, who had shaken down into a tight 'family' under their young commander. Although now beginning to suffer from dysentery through lack of proper diet, adequate fresh water or medical attention, they had seen what the enemy could throw at them, had seen friends die, mostly in ugly fashion, burning and screaming rather than through the kindly bullet in the head. They had learned to live with attack alarms in the small hours of the night when they had barely sunk into exhausted sleep after sweating to get their Panzer – now nicknamed 'One Eye' after a Russian shell had knocked away one of its headlights – ready for the next day's action. They were bruised and aching in every bone and sinew from the constant jolting and lacerated from falling against sharp metal edges. They smelt of sweat, smoke, grease and fear. Their smart black Panzer uniforms were salt and dust encrusted and splitting at the seams. They had discarded their ties in favour of strips of cloth to muffle their mouths and noses, bandit fashion, except when a Propaganda Company photographer headed in their direction. They were tired with a bone-weary ache which can only be appreciated by other combat soldiers who have been 'on the go' for a solid month. The Russians were not, despite the early gains, the pushover that the French had proven.

Fear was not conquered, but had become something else one learned to live with, like flaccid bowels and constant thirst, the ever-present dust which had taken over from weather as a topic of conversation, and the nauseating sway of the tank over the rough roads, the squeal of metal track links and the stench of exhaust and cordite fumes. Some of the men were religious despite the inroads National Socialism had made into Christianity, and for some of them this was sufficient. Others, like Meier, had to make their own mental adjustment. At least he had learned how to tackle the task at hand without the gut-wrenching sickness which had accompanied that first day in the line. He could eat. He could savour a plundered bottle of vodka with his crew without trying to dive inside it. He didn't duck every time a shell exploded nearby or cracked overhead, and instead of flinching when he heard the sound of a machine-gun, had trained himself to look around intelligently for its source. Most importantly, he had learned the knack of being able to fall asleep anywhere and at any time, dark dreamless sleeps of thankful oblivion until the next rude awakening. He had become a soldier in truth as well as in name.

Army Group South, as we have seen, might have been the strongest of the three but was faced with the strongest opposition, and the redeployment of Hoth's Panzergruppe IV to aid in the encirclement at Bialystock had slowed their own advance so that, by the end of May they were only just approaching Kiev, which Marshal Budenny had been furiously fortifying. With the Stalin line broached in three places in the south, at Zhitomir, west of Vinitsa and west of Pervomaisk, the canny Russian Marshal had realised that if the Germans were to be held at all it would be on the line of the River Dnieper, one of the Soviet Union's principal natural lines of defence. The inhabitants of Kiev had been press-ganged into digging extensive anti-tank ditches which German pioneers would have to bridge under fire before the Panzers could break through. The soldiery had similarly been busy digging revetments from behind which tanks could fire with only their turrets exposed. Reserves were being brought in from the Far East and the troops remaining in the west, including Kirponov's mechanised Corps, were fighting a gallant delaying action.

Feldmarschall von Bock knew that if Kirponov was allowed to escape, the resulting siege of Kiev would be a long and costly affair. Summoning Guderian and Rommel to his headquarters in Vinitsa on 7 June, von Bock outlined the situation. Panzergruppe IV could not be returned from its current position north of the Pripet Marshes in time to help Kirponov from escaping the net. Panzergruppen I and II would have to do it on their own, the former aiming to hook through Belaya Tserkov towards Novo Archangelsk from the north-west and the latter through Pervomaisk in a south-easterly direction towards the same objective. If they could move quickly enough, before Kirponos could react his six Corps could be encircled and trapped around Uman. The two motorised Waffen-SS divisions, *Das Reich* and *Wiking*, would lend their support.[4] Speed was of the essence.

'Off again,' Georg Meier told his crew after returning from an officers' Order Group on the evening of the 8th. 4th Panzer

Division, its tanks like all the other vehicles in the Panzer-gruppe marked with a white letter 'G' for Guderian, was part of the southerly prong of the new advance. The men had suffered considerable frustration over the last few days, striking at an enemy who often seemed to be invisible. There would be a local Russian counter-attack over the ripening grainfields, but by the time reinforcements were rushed to the spot, the Russians would have gone once more. The Luftwaffe was doing its best, but with so many thousands of square miles to search, its recon-naissance aircraft were not always able to spot enemy rede-ployments, especially when they took place at night. This maddening game of punch and counter-punch was only serving Russian purposes, by disrupting and slowing what should have been a decisive advance. It would be good to get moving pro-perly again.

Notes

1 The date and wording of this Directive are correct.

2 In actuality the main German drive was in the centre, but Hitler then diverted tanks and troops from this axis to help in the south, especially around Kiev where hundreds of thousands of Russian soldiers were taken prisoner. This weakened the central force so that, further handicapped by the onset of winter and the redeployment of Russian troops to bolster the capital's defences, the German forces were never able to seize the city.

3 This guaranteed such things as proper treatment for prisoners-of-war, Red Cross access, the right of captured officers to refuse to work, etc. In other words, dignified treatment for PoWs. In general, Germany aboce pretty well by the convention, although there were the same inevitable breaches as occurred in Allied camps for German prisoners – but by this Order Hitler made the Russians exempt and they suffered appallingly. German soldiers in Soviet hands fared no worse, however.

4 Although nominally independent of the Wehrmacht, the Waffen-SS divisions fell, by Hitler's directive, under Army operational control in the field.

6
Bermuda Triangle

Heydrich called me at four in the afternoon. 'Himmler's dead. Come to my house at seven this evening, and dust off your notes from July 1940.'

We all knew Himmler was dying, of course. After the grenade had exploded in his Mercedes while he was being driven to the Hradcany Palace during a tour of inspection in Prague at the end of May, he was a dead man. It would have taken a lot more than all the Führer's horses and men to put that evil, egg-headed, bespectacled old bastard back together, let alone physicians who only know how to use herbs and leeches. Leeches, for pity's sake! It's 1942 not 1642. Heydrich was de-lighted, of course. He should have been in the car at the time but had to stay at the palace to arrange the reception and await the Reichsführer's pleasure. Of course, he flew straight back to Berlin once the Führer's own doctor, Dr Gebhardt, arrived. He said the assassins had been killed in a shoot-out with the SS. They had hidden in a cellar which Heydrich had ordered flooded to make sure of them. I wonder why Heydrich wanted them so thoroughly dead? That's dangerous thinking. I know why he wanted to get back to Berlin so quickly, though. Himmler's files. Heydrich keeps files on everybody, that's why we're all so scared to cross him. So did Himmler, and Heydrich wanted them – especially his own – before that crass idiot Müller* or someone thought of them. Crafty bugger. But that's why he's managed to stay one jump ahead all this time. I wonder why he wants my 1940 notes though? He knows well enough what happened.

*Heinrich Müller, head of the Gestapo and an admirer of Stalin. Not for his politics, just for the way he carried things out.

I first met Heydrich while I was still a law student, and a relatively new member of the SS. I liked the class of people the SS
attracted, far better than those rowdies in the brownshirts, the
SA. Common, the lot of them. I didn't take part directly in the
Röhm purge, but I knew it was happening, of course. Good rid-
dance.

Heydrich's different from anyone. I must admit I was a bit
nervous when I got my first summons to meet him. He was
pleasant enough – we talked about music and the law, topics we
share in common. It was his eyes that got me, though, pale,
piercing, and his voice, rather too high pitched. It grated . . . it
still grates . . . and he stutters sometimes, something he tries
very hard to overcome in public. He's an elegant son of a bitch
too, that uniform always perfectly tailored to hide the width of
his hips and show off his long legs. He'd have made a beautiful
woman. Glad he'll never read this. I'm not giving him anything
for his files. I've done enough.

1940 though. What does he want those old files for? We tried
hard enough and it might even have worked. Ribbentrop*
called me over to his office 'at once' one morning. I told Heydrich,
of course, straight away. I know which side my bread's but-
tered. Then I got a car and went straight to the Foreign Office.

'Schellenberg, good to see you.' He stayed seated behind his
desk, leaving me standing at attention like a waxwork dummy.
He knew I'd been to Spain and Portugal on a couple of under-
cover do's, of course, but I didn't tell him anything he didn't
already know. He seemed a bit disappointed and then asked me
point-blank how well I knew the Duke of Windsor. I'd met him,
of course, on several occasions, although he probably wouldn't
remember them, and liked him for his understanding of people.
I felt sorry for him in a way – after all, not many of us have to
choose between a woman and a crown – but at the same time I
felt he had made the right decision for himself and the British
government had made the right decision for the country. Ribbentrop didn't like that. He said that Edward was virtually a
prisoner, spied on by his own people and desperate to escape.
He was, Ribbentrop said, a great admirer of the Führer and the
main reason he had abdicated was because he did not want to
see his own country dragged into a war with ours. I didn't

*Joachim Ribbentrop, German Foreign Minister from 1938.

believe him then and I still don't really. But, orders are orders and I knew I had to do what he asked – after I'd cleared my yardarm through Heydrich, of course. (He was in the Navy before he got thrown out after some affair with an Admiral's daughter, and still likes to use naval language even though there aren't many people in the SS who understand it. But he always likes to stay aloof and if some private language suits him, it doesn't bother me.)

Anyway, the upshot of the conversation was that Ribbentrop wanted me to visit the Duke in Spain and offer him fifty million Swiss Francs if he would move to Switzerland and disassociate himself from the actions of the rest of the Royal Family. I ask you! But there was better to come. If the Duke didn't go along with the idea I was to kidnap him and his wife – the word kidnap wasn't actually used, Ribbentrop likes circumlocutions. I was flabbergasted, and Ribbentrop saw it. He tried to cover up by saying that the kidnapping would really be to get the Duke away from the surveillance of SIS, the British Secret Intelligence Service, so that he could speak his own mind without coercion. 'Oh boy, Prinz Albrechtstrasse*,' I thought, 'even you don't get as devious as this.'

Ribbentrop could see I wasn't too happy with the deal so he dialled the Führer headquarters and within a moment I was listening on the extension to this exalted conversation. It ended with the Führer's words, 'He [meaning me] has all the authorisation he needs. Tell him from me that I am relying upon him.' There's no answer to that. I did what I was told like a good little boy . . . after telling Heydrich of course . . . and two days later flew out to Madrid.

It was hot, as usual, and I freshened up before going to the Embassy to see Eberhard von Stohrer, our Ambassador in Spain. He knew something of Ribbentrop's plan already. After all, he had provided most of the information for Ribbentrop in the first place. The Duke of Windsor, he said, was now living in Lisbon, and the problem was how to get him into Spain. Spain at that time, of course, was still neutral, despite pressure on Franco to join the Axis. But, thanks to the contribution our Condor Legion had made in helping him win the war against the Republicans, he was well disposed towards us and would,

*Gestapo headquarters.

von Stohrer said, help in any way short of letting the Spanish authorities be seen to be directly involved.

The Duke had been invited to a hunting party on an estate close to the border between Spain and Portugal, von Stohrer continued, but a date had not yet been fixed. I decided to go and study the lie of the land myself and after arranging accommodation with friends in Lisbon I took an Embassy car (it actually belonged to the Secret Service) and drove there with my two bodyguards. In Lisbon I had a long meeting with another old friend, an influential Japanese businessman, who promised to get me plans of the house where the Duke and Duchess were staying. I then paid my respects to our Ambassador, von Huene, who was as concerned as von Stohrer that nothing be done to upset Portuguese neutrality.

My Japanese friend was as good as his word and next day not only gave me detailed plans of the house in Estoril but also full details of the guards and the household routine. Within five days, spending Secret Service money lavishly, I had most of the Portuguese guards replaced by our own people and spotted a couple of informants amongst the servants.

It soon became obvious that, although the Duke was not happy with the post of Governor of Bermuda he had been offered, his allegiance was still clearly to England. This made any direct approach impossible. Moreover, it seemed he had decided not to take up the hunting invitation. But I was being pressed hard by telegrams from Ribbentrop to take action. 'The Führer orders that an abduction is to be organised at once.' What was I to do? The Ambassador was no help and even my Japanese friend baulked at the idea of physical action. British security had been stepped up and the ship which was to take the Duke to Bermuda was due to dock any day. In the event matters were taken out of my hands. The ship arrived before I could devise a plan and, although there was a bomb scare at one point, the Duke and Duchess sailed on schedule.

I was obviously anxious as to how my failure would be received back in Berlin but Ribbentrop, although rather offhand, said that the Führer agreed with my decisions. Heydrich told me it had been a harebrained scheme from the outset and that he thought I'd behaved rather shrewdly. That, it seemed, was that. Now Heydrich wanted to go over events again. I wondered why.

'Come in, Walter,' Heydrich greeted me when I arrived at his house promptly at seven. I still called him 'Sir' while on duty, but he'd mellowed enough to grant me first name status by this time. We went to his study, which was lined with books. When a white-jacketed servant had poured us a glass of wine each, he went to the wall safe and, turning his back obviously to prevent my seeing the combination, took out a slim file.

'Now,' he said. 'Heinie's files have produced something rather interesting. Before I go into that, though, I want you to tell me everything you can remember about the Duke of Windsor while you were in Lisbon, especially his attitude towards us.' (We always called Himmler 'Heinie' behind his back.)

I opened my briefcase and took out my notebook. 'No,' said Heydrich, leaning back in his leather chair and steepling his fingers, 'give me a personal rundown.'

I told him everything I could remember. That while the Duke had admired much of the reconstruction Hitler had achieved for Germany, he would not throw in his lot with us while Britain and Germany were at war. 'Suppose we were not?', Heydrich asked. It was clearly a metaphorical question for he leaned forward and continued, 'Britain is finished. The country is completely isolated now. The only convoys getting through are from Canada and America and our U-boats are sinking them at a rate the Brits can't possibly afford to sustain. The people are beginning to starve. Soon they *will* be starving.'

I knew this to be true from the reports which passed across my own desk. Despite an immense agricultural effort, Britain's own resources were not enough to feed the population at anything above a mere subsistence level. The wolf packs were taking an enormous toll and although they were suffering their own casualties now that more of the new British escort carriers were in service, the losses were still very one-sided. The tally for April was the highest ever. We were sinking ships faster than they could be built[1].

'Now,' Heydrich continued, 'we come to the file.' He tapped the folder on his desk. 'It appears we have an agent in the Governor's Residence in Hamilton [the capital of Bermuda].' This came as no real surprise to me. The Reich at this time had more intelligence networks than intelligence, it often seemed, and we were always tripping over each other's toes. Apart from our own outfit, the SD*, there was Admiral Canaris' *Abwehr* (military intelligence), the Gestapo, the criminal police and both Ribbentrop and Göring had their own setups. Probably there were others. Nor was it unusual to find that a man like Himmler had his own agent in place outside the normal SS framework.

'Britain is on her knees and most people are fed up with the war, but Churchill is as stubborn as a mule. Suppose the Duke of Windsor were to announce that he had managed to negotiate a peace which left the country with its honour? What then? How would the average Englishman react?'

I thought for a few moments. 'I think they would welcome it. There would be resentment, of course. Britain hasn't lost a war since the American secession. There would be a certain amount of anxiety. The Führer would have to be seen to be very generous. We'd have to do another Denmark[2].' I paused again. 'What about King George and the rest of the Royal Family though?'

'We would allow them to go to Canada. Edward would become King again. Don't forget that millions of people hated the fact that he was forced to abdicate. They'd welcome him back if he brought peace at the same time. We would offer help to rebuild the British cities and industries, build new homes, send them food. We might even let that fool Mosley become Gauleiter[3].'

I was lost in thought. It *could* work, I realised with sudden excitement. The British people knew they had done all the could. Few would have believed they could have held out for as long as they had. There was no dishonour in a negotiated peace. I said as much to Heydrich. 'Good. I'm glad you agree. Now, I want you to take a little pleasure cruise.'

A week later I was in Brest. The huge concrete U-boat pens, impervious to British bombing, were one of the finest achievements of the Todt Organisation and French slave labour. I was greatly impressed. I was not so enamoured at the thought of a voyage in a submarine. Although I don't normally suffer from claustrophobia, the thought of being trapped helplessly sixty-odd feet below the surface of the Atlantic in a tin coffin didn't appeal. Still, I hope I concealed my feelings as I was introduced to Kapitän Franz Poppe, captain of *U-109*. She was a long-

Sicherheitsdienst, the SS Secret Service. Walter Schellenberg was Heydrich's number two.

range Type IXB, 237 feet long and displacing around 1,200 tons which could travel 12,000 miles without refuelling. At ten knots the journey to Bermuda, where I was to be dropped offshore in a dinghy, would take about a fortnight depending on whether we had to take any avoiding action from British shipping. Although *U-109* had six torpedo tubes, we weren't looking for trouble on this trip.

As it turned out, the voyage was uneventful. There was one false alarm when a lookout mistook a bird for an aircraft and we crash-dived, but apart from that nothing except the damp monotony. At least submariners eat well. I had thought I might be seasick but the queasiness of the first few hours after we slipped from Brest on the high tide shortly after midnight on 15 June soon passed away and I put it down to nerves. Kapitän Poppe proved an amiable fellow and knowledgeable, and I enjoyed our talks when we surfaced at night and could relax. As we approached the islands, of course, the tension was greater, for we did not know what warships might be present, and we stayed at periscope depth except when we had to surface to recharge the batteries.

We closed the islands on the first day of the new month, two years almost to the day since I had flown to Madrid. The submarine surfaced into a balmy tropical night, the stars more brilliant than I had ever seen them. A passing thought struck me. Now that Himmler was dead, we wouldn't be lumbered with any more of this astrological nonsense. Hitler had hated astrologers with the same venom he showed to Jews ever since Hess had defected in May the previous year; a strange reversal in a man who had hitherto relied on them. But where was I? Oh yes. Opening a deck hatch, crewmen passed out the inflatable rubber dinghy and blew it up with a cylinder of compressed air. One sailor held the boat steady while I climbed in after thanking Poppe warmly. He was to remain indefinitely on station a few miles off the coast until I reported back using the radio which Himmler's agent had hidden. None of us knew how long this delicate mission was going to take.

Two crewmen rowed me to a sandy beach, the last few moments an exhilarating ride through breaking surf which glinted like liquid diamonds. They pulled the boat ashore to let me get out, for someone walking around in the small hours of the morning with soaking wet shoes and trousers would be bound to arouse some suspicion. I carried no suitcase, only papers identifying me as a Spanish businessman and, hidden in the lining of my lightweight jacket, more genuine credentials in the form of a formal proposal signed by Hitler which I would give the Duke if an initial approach showed that he might be favourably disposed to listen to us. The two sailors pushed the dinghy back into the surf and began paddling away. I was quite alone on a pure white beach. The war seemed a lightyear away.

The beach on which I had been landed was about five miles outside Hamilton, and my contact lived on the outskirts of the town so I trudged up the beach, found the narrow road and started walking. It was very pleasant and for the present I had not a care in the world. Tomorrow would look after itself. The air was pleasantly warm, a slight sea breeze rustling the palms and sweet-smelling bougainvillaeas.

My first surprise was that the contact was a woman. I reached the correct address without having seen another soul shortly before first light and rapped on the insect screen over the back door. A few moments passed, then a voice unmistakenly English asked, 'Who is it?'. I gave the expected reply – 'A friend from abroad' (how I loathe these silly passwords!) – and she replied, 'You must have had a long swim'. 'All the way from the Unter den Linden you silly bitch, now open the door.' The room was in darkness and I stumbled slightly as I went in. 'It's safe to have a light,' she said, suiting action to words by lighting a match, removing the mantle and putting the flame to the wick of the hurricane lamp. 'I often have to start work early so no-one will remark if I'm up and about now.' This was my second surprise. She was extraordinarily beautiful even in the dim light, long dark hair haloing a slender face with slightly wistful eyes. She was only wearing a cotton housecoat, and her face was puffy with sleep. I instantly regretted my earlier harsh words.

'Schellenberg,' I said formally, extending my hand. Then came the third surprise. She laughed. You don't often hear women laugh. They giggle or gurgle. This was a deep, rich laugh which reached the eyes. 'How formal, Herr Schellenberg,' she said, lowering her eyes in mock demureness. 'I'm Siobhan.' The Irish name, pronounced so correctly 'Sh-vaun' in that faultless English accent, threw me even further. Who was this witch, and where had Himmler found her? The file Heydrich had appropriated had given no clues, just the name 'S.A. Manners', codename 'Juniper', address and radio frequency, date of recruitment (1940) and a scribbled note in Himmler's spidery script, 'reliable'.

'Please, sit down,' she invited, gesturing vaguely at the half-dozen canework easy chairs scattered about the room. 'Would you like some coffee – *real* coffee?' 'Thank you,' I said lamely, 'that would be very nice.' I was ashamed of my tongue. Normally I like to think I am pretty fluent with women, and I know Heydrich and I have had some wild times when the mood struck him. In the presence of this woman, for some reason, I was tongue-tied.

She went into the kitchen and put a pot on top of the banked stove, then came back into the main room. 'So, Herr Schellenberg,' she said – and did I detect mockery in her voice? – 'how is Berlin?' We made small talk while the coffee boiled and I rediscovered my tongue. She was fascinated by my description of Hanna Reitsch, whom I had met recently at Hitler's birthday reception. 'Oh, I would love to fly,' she said spontaneously, clapping her hands like a child. I put her age in the mid-twenties. 'That could be arranged – when we get this business over,' I said, understanding her enthusiasm for I, too, love to fly, and Hanna Reitsch was not only one of Hitler's favourites but a first-class test pilot to boot.

The coffee was as delicious as only real coffee can be when you have been drinking muck mixed with ground acorns for months, and I sipped appreciatively. 'Oh!', she exclaimed suddenly, looking at her watch as the brilliant dawn sunlight began flooding into the room, 'I must get dressed for work. We will have to talk later. I will be back at lunchtime. If there is anything you want, look in the kitchen.' She showed me the room I was to sleep in and the toilet, actually an 'inside' one rather than the more usual privvy. 'It might be best if you don't go outside today,' she said. 'I wasn't sure exactly when you were arriving so I must prepare the ground.'

At that moment sleep, in a bed rather than a rolling bunk, was what I suddenly felt I needed more than anything else, so after Siobhan had left on her bicycle I washed and relaxed in unaccustomed luxury. My last conscious thought was of those eyes, framed in that fragrant bouquet of hair.

It was the smell of cooking which awoke me, a delicious aroma of curried chicken. I found Siobhan in the kitchen, her hair tied back in a band, sweat dripping down her nose. I noticed that she did not follow American fashion and left her armpits unshaved, Continental fashion. For some reason this gave me obscure pleasure. Then I realised that I was thinking far too much of Siobhan – and I still didn't know whether 'Manners' was 'Miss' or Mrs'. There was no sign of a wedding band, though. It took a conscious effort to direct my mind to the business at hand.

The curry was delicious, brightened with chopped banana and grated coconut, and I sounded Siobhan out on her background, trying not to sound like an SS interrogator. Yet I knew my life could depend on this woman, and even Himmler's scribbled note did not reassure me totally.

We swapped life stories. There was no friction but I was alert for a word out of place, a momentary hesitation which would reveal a lie – or a concealed truth. I told her of my early years in Saarbrücken, where my father made pianos, and how that had later led to a rapport with Heydrich which few shared. Of our move to Luxembourg while I was in my early teens, then university at Bonn, where I studied medicine for a while before turning to the law. Then the discovery that, in order to get anywhere after 1933 – when Hitler became Chancellor – you really had to be a member of the National Socialist Party, and preferably the SS.

In return she told me of her own early life in that little fishing village of Dundalk on the eastern coast of Ireland, so beloved of writers and artists. Of her father's and her grandfather's hatred of the English for all they had done to Ireland, and something of the parts both had played in the Easter Uprising. 'My name wasn't Manners then, of course,' she said reflectively. 'I met a young man – he was training to be a solicitor, like you – and we fell in love. We married in 1938 and he was killed in 1940.' She wasn't looking at me any longer, instead seeing things outside this room a world and perhaps a lifetime away. 'The British soldiers came across the border – we had moved to a cottage just outside the village then. They were looking for IRA men who were helping German agents get into England through Liverpool.

'I knew Alan – that was my husband – was often away on

sudden business trips, but I didn't know he had anything to do
with the Republicans. Then that night these three soldiers suddenly burst into the house. They kicked the door in while we
were in bed.' I put my hand over hers but she didn't seem to
react, being lost in a horrifying nightmare. 'I screamed but
they ignored me and pulled Alan out of bed. They dragged him
down the stairs and I heard him shouting in anger. Then there
was a thud, and Alan screamed.' I nodded without letting go of
her hand. I'd seen and heard plenty of the same in Berlin and
other parts. Her words wouldn't stop now, though. 'He kept
screaming and I kept hearing these thuds. The soldiers were
asking him questions. I couldn't hear what they were, but they
were kicking him you know.' I knew. 'Then there was an awful
crunching noise and the screams stopped but there was a horri-
ble bubbling noise.' They'd broken his nose or jaw, or both.
'Then it all went quiet. I didn't know whether to move or what
to do. As I said, the cottage was a fair way out of the village and
... I hadn't any clothes on anyway. Then the soldiers came back
upstairs. They called me things like "whore" and other words I
didn't understand, and then they ... they ...'

'It's all right Siobhan. It's all right. I understand.' I did, too.
Threaten someone's life, maim and mutilate him, subject him
to the worst he can imagine, and if he's strong enough, sometimes he'll hold out. Not often, but sometimes. When that hap-
pens, you turn to victim number two. If they're close, you can
often get one to spill the beans rather than watch their wife or
husband get knocked around. Those English soldiers were
obvious louts who didn't understand the first thing about inter-
rogation. Instead they killed the man, raped the woman and
left with no information at all. No wonder they were losing the
war.

'That's what turned you against them?' The question was
meaningless, really, her tears were flowing freely now. Cathar-
sis. 'How did Himmler get on to you, and how on earth did you
end up in Bermuda?' I had to get at the truth quickly, while she
was still wrapped in remembered pain and grief.

'I went to Sean. He had been one of my father's friends and I
knew he was something to do with the Republicans because he
and my father used to sit up talking at night after I'd been sent
to bed. I saw him the next morning and told him what had happened. I didn't want to go to the *Garda* – the police – and Sean

said that was exactly right. "We'll find the bastards who did
your Alan in, he said. "Best the police think it was us that killed
him. That'll turn any suspicion away from you." He thought for
a moment. "Yes, that'll work very nicely," he said to himself. I
didn't know what he meant, then, of course. "You go and see
Doc Brodie, Siobhan. As far as he knows, or anyone else, Alan
didn't come home last night. You never saw him. Three men in
masks broke into the house, not soldiers. All right? Think you
can manage that?" I nodded. I was still feeling numb – shock, I
suppose. I saw the doctor and he said I hadn't actually been
hurt. I just felt filthy. When I got home, Alan's body had gone.
Sean took me later to where they had buried him. Doc Brodie
reported to the police and they came and talked to me about the
rape. When they asked where Alan was, I said in Dublin on
business. They knew he travelled a lot, you see, so they weren't
suspicious of that. They said they'd contact him and get him to
come home.'

   'Of course, they couldn't find him, so there were more questions, but in the end he was simply listed as missing. That hap-
pens in Ireland, you know.' 'In Germany too,' I said. 'Sean
looked after me. I didn't want to go back to the cottage again,'
she continued, more composed now. 'It was about three weeks
later that the stranger arrived. Sean just introduced him as
John. I knew he wasn't Irish though, or English for that matter.
He had a slightly funny accent that I couldn't place at the time,
although later I learned that he was German. That first time I
think he just wanted to get a look at me because he didn't say
anything about himself, just asked me about myself and my
family, how I felt after what had happened to Alan and me,
things like that.'

   'A few days later he returned. This time he told me that he
was a German intelligence officer working directly for Reichsführer Himmler. He also said that the Germans were helping
the Republicans, smuggling them guns and money to fight
against the common enemy, England. Would I, he asked, be
prepared to help as well. I didn't hesitate, but I said I didn't
think I could fire a gun. He smiled and said that wouldn't be
necessary. That I could pass as an Englishwoman anywhere,
and that was how I could be useful to them. My parents had
sent me to Roedean, you see.' So that explained that.

   The rest of the story was familiar. A month on a farm deep in the country where Siobhan was taught how to use a radio and the basics of codes and cyphers while a cover identity was built for her, retaining her own name so that she would not be caught out if she unexpectedly bumped into an acquaintance. Then a period waiting for an assignment. That came in August, after the Duke of Windsor had arrived in Bermuda. She was provided with tickets for passage on a ship, money to open a bank account and a radio which was smuggled on and off the vessel by a crewman. She settled down in a small house as an Englishwoman whose husband had been killed at Dunkirk, a common enough story. Her task was that of a 'sleeper'. Himmler didn't want her to report on ship movements or anything like that, and in fact she was told specifically not to use the radio or do anything else to draw attention to herself. So she settled into the peaceful life of the island and within a couple of months had managed to get a job as a companion to the Duchess of Windsor in the Governor's Residence in Hamilton.

As had happened in Lisbon, she was able to give me detailed plans of the house and its routine. There were guards, but they were relaxed, there was none of the tight security there had been earlier. She said that the Duchess often talked about the war. She wasn't anti-British, Siobhan said, but often said things which made her believe both the Duke and Duchess would like to see an end to the war and a return to normality. We decided that my best chance was to try to talk to the Duke at the next reception. Siobhan could get 'Carlos Santiago', Spanish businessman, an invitation.

So it happened. Ten days or so later we went to the Residence together. By this time we were sleeping together. I wasn't sure whether I was in love with her, but she was beautiful, intelligent and it was only natural that a young woman who had been widowed for two years should seek male companionship. Hamilton society was quite relaxed about such things so long as one was discreet, and we enjoyed dining out in one of the little waterfront restaurants which served such delicious fish and chicken dishes. There were no food shortages here.

The reception was typical of such affairs. I had been to many in Berlin. Monkey-jacketed waiters circulated with silver trays of champagne. The only difference between them and their counterparts in Germany was that they were black. The male guests were elegant in white tropical suits, their ladies like butterflies in brightly coloured dresses. There were few men in uniform.

The Duke received us as we were announced: 'Mr Carlos Santiago and Mrs Siobhan Manners'. This was the first time I had seen him since before the war and I doubted strongly whether he would recognise me. I was shocked to see how much he had aged, though. He enquired politely into my business – Siobhan had already briefed the Duchess so the Duke knew who I was supposed to be. I commented on the difficulties the war had created for honest businessmen and he sighed. 'This war, this terrible war. If only I knew how it could be brought to an end.' Then he turned to speak to the next arrivals and Siobhan took me round the room to talk to some of her other friends and acquaintances. I was elated. I could not have hoped for such a positive reaction. I became convinced that my mission must succeed.

I didn't get another opportunity to talk to the Duke that day but listening to other people talking provided useful background. Many seemed convinced that we had bitten off more than we could chew by invading Russia, but that any reprieve would be too late for England. Several people asked me, believing me a Spaniard, whether I thought General Franco would come into the war on Germany's side. I simply told the truth as I saw it, that Franco was playing a waiting game while he struggled to rebuild an economy shattered by three years of civil war, and certainly didn't want to enter another major conflict. I didn't mention the Spanish volunteers who had already come forward to form the so-called Blue Division to fight on our side in Russia since I didn't know whether that was still supposed to be secret.

The reception over, we went back to Siobhan's house, made love, ate a leisurely meal and sat talking quietly. Now that contact had been established, I had to find a way of speaking to the Duke privately. That problem resolved itself in an unexpected fashion. Next day, when Siobhan returned from work, she said that the Duke had asked her more about me and ended by saying he would like to talk to me further. Could I be at the Residence at eleven the following morning for coffee?

When I arrived, I was surprised to be ushered straight into the Duke's study. He invited me to sit and joined me across the coffee table, already laid with cups and a steaming jug. A servant poured for both of us, then left quietly. A strange sense of déjà vu overcame me. The Duke eyed me keenly. 'Berlin, 1936,' he said. 'You weren't Spanish then, and your name isn't Santiago. I could have had you arrested, but I'm intrigued. Why are you here? I don't believe you've come to assassinate me, such an act could not benefit Germany any more, if it ever could have. So there has to be another reason.'

'You're right, sir, of course,' I said. 'My name is Schellenberg, Walter Schellenberg, and I am here at the express orders of the Führer and the head of the SS Secret Service. For the moment they are the only two people who know why.' I stood up, the coffee untouched at this unexpected development. I had been given my opportunity, now could I carry it off?

'The Führer has never sought war with England,' I continued. The Duke nodded. 'Your island is isolated as it has never before been isolated. Our U-boats are sinking your ships faster than they can be built. Our troops have taken Egypt and Palestine and South Africa has seceded. You know all this, of course, sir.' It was natural to call him 'sir', you couldn't do anything else. He had the sort of dignity which only centuries of breeding can produce. 'Now look at England itself. The people barely get enough to eat as it is. Your industries are hamstrung for want of raw materials.' I went through all the arguments Heydrich and I had put together so carefully.

'The Führer wishes to make peace but King George and Churchill will not let him. We are engaged in a war to destroy communism, not England. If you would return millions of Englishmen and women would welcome you. We would guarantee the personal safety of your family and give them escort to whichever country they chose to live in – Canada perhaps, or even here. We will guarantee English civil liberties within the bounds necessary to maintain law and order. The English parliament would continue to be wholly autonomous in dealing with domestic affairs. There will be no army of occupation unless there is armed resistance. South African goods would once more flow into your ports unhindered, as will those from the other Commonwealth countries – and, of course, from Europe again.'

I reached into my jacket pocket. 'I have everything in writing here, sir,' I said, handing him the bulky white envelope. 'There is a translation as well.'

The Duke took the envelope. There was anguish in his face now. He lit a cigarette and stared at the floor. 'It's too much,' he said finally. 'I can't give you a decision now. It's my country at war, and I can't betray it. But which is the greater betrayal? To end this hopeless war or to sit uselessly here stagnating in the sun?' He looked up. 'I can't give you an answer now, Schellenberg.' I nodded my understanding. 'I need to talk to my wife. She's American, you know. She has a different perspective in these things. Where can I get in touch with you? At Mrs Manners'?'

He stood up. 'Thank you, Schellenberg,' he said. 'I'll let you know when I've read this,' he gestured to the envelope on the table. He extended his hand. It was firm and dry. A servant showed me out.

Four weeks later the Duke of Windsor broadcast to the English nation from Berlin. His disappearance from Bermuda had caused shockwaves through the Empire. Abduction? Murder? An accident? Now the truth was out. Two days later King George VI abdicated and the broad terms of an armistice were agreed, Ribbentrop flying to London with an entourage of senior officers and officials. The official cessation of hostilities took place at midnight on 8 August 1942. German troops began arriving the following morning to disarm the British Army. The arrests soon followed. Churchill and the other members of the War Cabinet were put on trial for war crimes and sentenced to execution in the Tower of London. The Royal Family sailed for Canada. Now the reconstruction could begin.

Siobhan and I returned to Ireland to see her family. The Führer had congratulated us both personally, his face wreathed with smiles. A month later we were married. It was one of the finest weddings Berlin had ever seen.

Notes

1 April 1942 was historically the high spot for the U-boats. After this their success rate began to decline. With South Africa out of the war, their effect would have been far greater.

2 Although Denmark had been invaded in 1940, its government, police and other institutions had been left untouched and of all the Occupied countries, it enjoyed the highest level of freedom within the Greater Reich, for Hitler considered the Danes 'Aryan'.

3 Germany was organised into administrative regions called *Gaus*, each headed by a *Gauleiter*, a political appointment equivalent to a General in the Army.

7
Stalingrad the Goal

The sight of three whole Panzer divisions on the march is really quite something, mused Conrad Hartstein as he skilfully piloted the little high-winged Fieseler Storch five thousand feet above the seemingly endless steppes. 'The biggest traffic jam since the Berlin Olympics, I reckon, sir,' he shouted to his passenger. Heinz Guderian grinned and nodded. Conversation was difficult in the aircraft at the best of times. Unlike Rommel, who usually piloted himself, Guderian had never learned more than the rudiments of flying so had to rely on a 'chauffeur'.

At full strength – which the divisions in the Panzergruppe fell far short of by this stage in the campaign – a German armoured division contained over 3,000 vehicles: tanks, self-propelled guns, armoured cars, half-tracks, recovery vehicles, trucks, cars and motor cycles, plus the towed field, anti-aircraft and anti-tank guns. In single file on a road such a column would stretch for fifteen miles or more, and deployed for action would occupy a front up to five miles wide. Somewhere down there, an insignificant speck amongst thousands of others, was Georg Meier's Panzer III.

Meier was feeling elated as the advance resumed, because he had just received his promotion to Oberleutnant and had been given command of the 3rd Company's 2nd Troop of five tanks*. The boy from Eisenach had come a long way.

The tanks threw up vast columns of dust which gave the daylight a sombre cast. Fully refuelled and with their ammunition racks filled to capacity with 78 rounds of 50 mm shells, the Panzer IIIs had a cross-country range of just over sixty miles,

---

*In theory, but not always in practice, there were three Troops to a Panzer Company, four Companies to a Battalion and two Battalions to a Regiment.

which meant they would have to refuel before reaching Per-vomaisk. Of the enemy so far there was no sign but they were out there somewhere. Guderian's pilot banked the light air-craft steeply as it passed over the leading wedge of tanks. Al-though there was so far no evidence of the Russians' presence, he had learned a healthy respect for the accuracy of their anti-aircraft fire. Moreover, although the Luftwaffe still had aerial supremacy, Soviet fighters were being encountered in greater numbers now, and the Storch was unarmed. The speed with which the Russians had moved much of their industry east, out of range of all German bombers except the He 177 which was still only available in small numbers, showed their resilience and determination not to succumb.

The first signs of resistance came after the Panzers had ad-vanced about fifteen miles, when anti-tank guns opened up on 5th Panzer Division from concealed positions in a wood which the tanks had bypassed. Two vehicles were hit instantly, and the echelon nearest the wood swung to present the tanks' thicker frontal armour towards the threat. High explosive shells from the Panzer IIIs' 50 mm and Panzer IVs' 75 mm guns began falling amongst the trees. The divisional commander, General Gustav Fehn, radioed for Luftwaffe support and twenty minutes later three flights of Stukas appeared, un-leashing their 250 kg bombs over the Russian position. One by one the guns fell silent and 5th Panzer Division resumed its advance, speeding up to retrieve ground lost to the 4th and 20th.

Shortly afterwards the first Russian tanks were seen. Kir-ponov had become aware of his danger and knew that not only was he in danger of being encircled, but also that Guderian's Panzergruppe and the following infantry were driving a dangerous wedge across the neck of the Crimea, with its vital port of Sevastopol; Odessa, on the Black Sea coast further west, was already under siege by the 11th Army. As the Soviet T-34s careened through the waist-high grain, high velocity shells pumping from their 76 mm guns, the German tanks responded fiercely while heavy half-tracks raced up with their towed 88 mm guns. Men leapt from the vehicles and disengaged the heavy towing bars, then the guns were lowered onto their cruciform platforms, their wheeled limbers being shoved hastily out of the way. The barrel clamps were removed and the guns traversed onto their targets while the loaders formed a human chain from the ammunition stowage lockers in the backs of the half-tracks to the breeches. Soon the heavier 'crump' of these formidable weapons was added to the sharper 'crack' of the tanks' guns.

The Panzers found the situation reversed compared to the situation which had prevailed in the desert campaign. There, the lightly armed British tanks had to get in close in order to inflict any damage on the Panzers. Now they in turn had to close with the T-34s. Meier ordered his Troop forward at full speed, 25 mph, the tanks' engines straining under the load. There was no need for binoculars, the horizon seemed full of Russian tanks. 'Fire at will!', he shouted into the radio, and the interiors of the Panzers soon became blistering cocoons of heat and smoke. There was a resounding thump and the tank lurched suddenly to the left. A lucky shot had hit the axle of the front driving wheel on that side and the broken track flailed dangerously like a wounded snake. 'Everybody out!', Meier commanded, suiting action to words by leaping out of the turret. While his crew, fortunately all uninjured, sheltered behind the disabled vehicle, Meier raced across to his number two tank, commanded by Unteroffizier Fritz Maschlin. Fritz had seen what had happened and ordered his driver to stop. Meier swung himself onto the engine plates behind the turret. 'Room for a small one?', he shouted. Fritz was already levering himself out of the cupola. 'All yours, Georg!' Meier resumed command of his Troop, while Maschlin clung to the rear of the wildly swaying turret. Moments later his own tank was avenged, and he watched with satisfaction as a T-34 rocked back on its heels and exploded. By one of those lucky shots which happened far more often than might be believed, Maschlin's gunner had scored a direct hit on the Russian tank's gun barrel just as it also fired, the combined impact of the two shells bursting the barrel into twisted shards.

The battle lasted two hours, during which Meier had to change tanks a second time as a Russian shell penetrated the front compartment of Maschlin's vehicle. By a miracle, only the driver was killed but the radio operator was severely wounded in the head. Then the tanks on both sides began withdrawing one by one, seemingly almost by mutual consent, out of fuel, ammunition or both. The respite was only momentary for already the refuelling tanker trucks and ammunition carriers were lurching over the steppes towards the Panzers. Then it was back into the fray, the noise, the smell, the heat, dust and smoke almost unbearable. But eventually the Panzers prevailed, although sadly depleted in numbers. Kirponov pulled in his horns. The counter-attack had failed and he would have to try for a weaker spot.

The 4th Panzer Division reached Pervomaisk as dusk was beginning to fall at ten o'clock that night, having travelled over eighty miles and fought an exhausting battle since dawn. The town showed all the signs of a hasty evacuation, and abandoned 76 mm field guns littered the streets. Rebored to the standard German 75 mm calibre, these would become valuable dual-purpose anti-tank and field guns for the Wehrmacht.

In the north, Rommel's Panzergruppe had made equally good progress but also suffered losses as Soviet troops tried to break out eastwards from the closing armoured pincers. Feldmarschall von Bock had reason to be pleased with the day's progress though, and the following day the trap sprang shut as leading elements of General Graf von Esebeck's 2nd Panzer Division linked up with Horst Stumpff's 20th. Infantry units moving up from the west completed the encirclement of a huge pocket hundreds of square miles in extent. Kirponos himself was killed two days later leading a final attempt at a breakout with his remaining tanks, supported by infantry who charged suicidally in waves right into the mouths of the German machine-guns. It was a last throw. First individually and then in droves, the Russian soldiers began surrendering as the German forces tightened the noose. Nearly half a million Soviet soldiers entered captivity, forming huge columns of footsore humanity as they were forced to walk westwards to add their strength to Hitler's slave labour machine. It was the single biggest Russian disaster of the campaign so far, and recriminations rang around the Kremlin. Marshal Budenny was recalled and the defence of Kiev entrusted to Marshal Semyon Timoshenko, former Commissar of Defence with special responsibility for recruitment and training. Stalin permitted Budenny to live, but he was never again entrusted with a field command.

The two Panzergruppen now separated again, Rommel heading for Kremenchug, which lay at the narrows between two lakes on the River Dnieper, to force a crossing and attack Kiev from the south-east, where the defences were weakest. Mean-

(*above left*) Walter Koch bandaged after receiving a slight head wound; (*right*) General Kurt Student, founding father of the German parachute force; (*below*) Bomber's eye view of Grand Harbour and Valetta.

(*left*) Parachutes blossom over the defenders' heads; (*above*) Anxious mountain troops await their turn to board the Ju 52s; (*below*) German paras with British prisoners.

(*top left*) A Panzer III advancing at speed through the desert; (*bottom left*) The British cruiser tanks with their two-pounder guns were no match for the Panzers; (*above*) Even the new Panzer IIIs with 50mm guns were sometimes defeated, however; (*below*) An 88mm gun in action against British tanks.

(*above*) Rommel in his captured British Dorchester armoured command
vehicle christened 'Mammut'; (*below*) Victorious German troops enter
Cairo.

Himmler inspects the guard at the Hradcany Palace shortly before his assassination. Heydrich is on his right.

Master of intrigue – Reinhard Heydrick.

(*above*) A U-boat returns to Brest after a successful mission; (*below*) A massive aerial armada preceeded the invasion of Russia; these are Heinkel He 111s . . . and this is one of their victims (*top right*), a Russian Polikarpov fighter caught on the ground; (*bottom right*) Assault pioneers cross a Russian river.

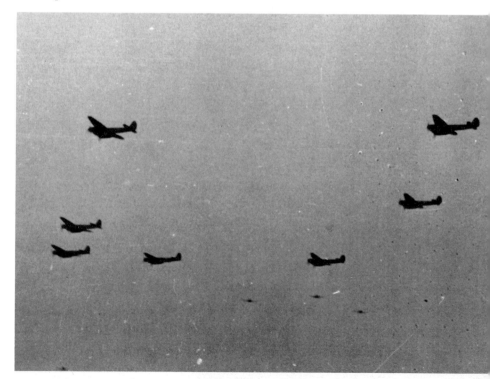

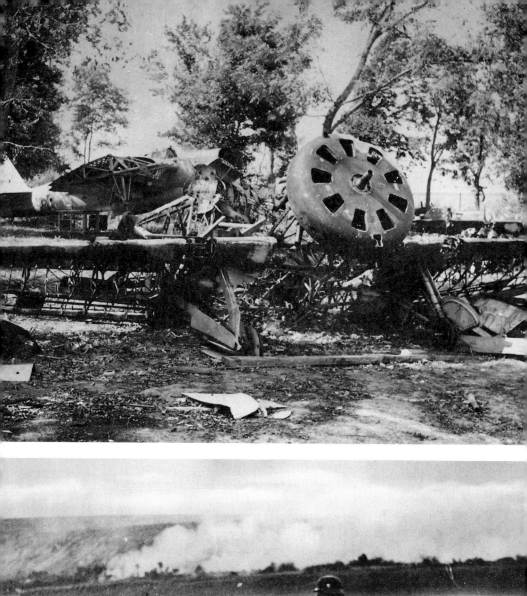

(*top left*) Panzers roll. View from Georg Meier's Panzer III during the advance; (*bottom left*) Knocked-out Soviet T-34s; (*below*) The German anti-tank gunners worked closely with the tanks and Russian armour burns.

Abandoned Russian 76mm guns which would soon find their way into German army service.

A glass of milk for an SS grenadier from a Ukranian farmer's wife.

(*above*) A Panzer III 'Special' like Georg Meier's undergoing maintenance; (*below*) SS General Jürgen Stroop arrives in Jerusalem.

(*top left*) An incredulous war correspondent listens with delight to the news of Britain's capitulation; (*bottom left*) Hitler and Göring congratulate Hanna Reitsch on being the first human being into space; (*above*) The new Tiger tanks arrive; (*below*) A tank commander surveys the Stalingrad horizon.

(*above*) Japanese troops move a field gun into position; (*below*) A grateful Führer with shipyard construction workers.

while Guderian struck across country towards Krivoi Rog and ultimately the important industrial city of Dnepropetrovsk, a hundred miles further east but also on the winding Dnieper.

While all this was happening, Nehring's Panzer Armee Afrika, now re-christened Panzer Armee Naher Osten (Middle East) had invaded Syria at the beginning of May. The only surviving British forces in the area apart from stragglers were Freyberg's New Zealand Division and the Indian Infantry Brigade which had escaped the debacle at El Alamein and made the nightmare trek across the Sinai Desert. Their escape had only been made possible because the German tanks and their crews were totally exhausted and unable to pursue. However, after a period of recuperation in Cairo and the fleshpots of Alexandria and Port Said, they were refreshed, while new supplies of tanks, guns and other equipment poured into Egypt to bring the divisions back up to strength.

Nehring had invaded Palestine in March, helped by uprisings in Iraq and Vichy French Syria inspired by the Mufti of Jerusalem, who had been forced into exile in Baghdad by the British because of his pro-German and anti-semitic policies. The revolt was led in military terms by the French General Henri Dentz, whom the British had defeated almost exactly a year earlier. Rashid Ali, the anti-British Iraqi leader who had similarly been forced into exile in Persia at about the same time, after British, Indian and Australian forces had subdued the country and retaken the principal airfields, also reappeared on the scene, more vociferous than ever. Field Marshal Alexander, the newly appointed British C-in-C Middle East, therefore found himself between the devil and the deep blue sea, an Arab revolt in the east and the advancing Panzers from the west. It was impossible to maintain law and order in Palestine, let alone defend the country, so as Panzer Armee Naher Osten crossed the Gaza Strip, Alexander evacuated Jerusalem and withdrew his forces to the easily defensible Golan Heights, on the border with Syria. Despite the Arab revolt, Damascus was still firmly in British hands so supplies were no problem for the time being, while Jordan remained pro-British and would resist any German attempt to outflank the position.

Alexander's main lack was heavy equipment, because few of the Eighth Army's tanks had survived the long crawl back from Alamein and many guns had had to be abandoned in the desert because the breakdown rate among the trucks was such that they could not all be towed away. Morale was also low, inevitably after such a succession of defeats and with no real prospect of relief. Moreover, there had been several incidents in which Arab zealots had murdered and mutilated Allied soldiers, either catching individuals on their way back to their barracks or throwing hand grenades into popular bars and restaurants.

German troops entered Jerusalem on 24 March 1942 and restored the Mufti to power. The Arab inhabitants welcomed them as liberators, but the remaining Jewish population was understandably apprehensive (many had already fled across the West Bank into comparatively liberal Jordan). They had a right to be afraid, for SS General Jürgen Stroop arrived with orders to establish one part of the city as a Jewish ghetto, as had been done in Warsaw. There, 400,000 Jews had been walled within a self-contained 'city' barely large enough to contain half the number, thousands of them existing on a single meagre bowl of rotten cabbage soup a day. Now the same was to be done with Jerusalem's 90,000 Jews*, half of them already refugees from Nazi Germany and its satrapies.

The average German soldier cared little for the 'Jewish question' and had only scanty knowledge of the 'final solution', the extermination camps. Large numbers had Jewish friends or acquaintances back in Germany – the local street corner shopkeeper, the old lady in the basement flat next door, people they had been at school with. Could these same people really be the threat the Führer said they were and Goebbels' propaganda kept ramming down their throats? But the wise man kept his mouth shut. 'Befehl ist Befehl' – an order is an order – and it took a brave and foolhardy individual to query orders in the nine year-old Thousand Year Reich.

Acting himself on orders from OKW, Nehring allowed Alexander and the remaining Allied forces in the Golan Heights to stew in their own juice for a month. He had been summoned back to Berlin after the fall of Jerusalem to receive his own accolade from the Führer and the coveted Field Marshal's baton. Rommel and Kesselring had made victory in the Mediterranean possible, but the capture of Palestine, heart of

*This is nearly triple the figure it had been twenty years earlier.

the Christian as well as the Jewish faith, had been very dear to Hitler's own heart and to the successful field commander, as usual, went the spoils. Nehring had also been informed of the impending invasion of Russia and given the same date of 1 May for the beginning of his final assault on the Allied positions in the Golan Heights.

The Allies had the advantage of rugged, boulder-strewn mountainous terrain with narrow, winding tracks which passed for roads to assist the defence. It was hardly ideal tank country, and Nehring therefore created a special battlegroup for this one operation, Kampfgruppe Crüwell, which basically consisted of the 90th Light Division reinforced by all the Panzer IVs from the 7th, 15th and 21st Panzer Divisions. A few Sturmgeschutz IIIs (assault guns) had also arrived via Haifa during the build-up period, and these were entrusted to the attack as well. (Unlike tanks, the assault guns did not have a revolving turret but instead a long-barrelled 75 mm gun in a fixed superstructure. They also had thicker armour than the Panzer IVs, 50 compared to 30 mm, and presented a lower profile which was less vulnerable to enemy anti-tank guns.)

Kampfgruppe Crüwell launched its attack over the Bnot Ya'akov Bridge across the River Jordan at the same time as the Panzers began to roll in Poland, although the men's watches read an hour earlier because of the difference in longitude. They could not hope to approach unobserved, because the Indians and New Zealanders in their positions around Nafekh could see for tens of miles. At the same time, though, the balance of the three Panzer divisions, together with the Italian *Ariete* armoured and *Trieste* motorised divisions, began heading out along the El Al road south of the Sea of Galilee towards Rafid, so as to cut off the Allied retreat on the relatively open plain. A huge demonstration was beginning to form up in Damascus at the same time so as to clog the roads and keep the British security forces occupied.

The initial assault went badly wrong. Crüwell's troops, although outnumbering the defenders, had to advance uphill, exposing themselves to enemy fire from concealed positions. It was rather like Greece all over again. The British tanks were at a disadvantage, because they could not depress their gun barrels sufficiently while firing from hull-down positions so had to expose themselves, fire and retreat. The Panzers had their own problems as well, though, because it is notoriously difficult to aim accurately at an uphill target. The battle turned, therefore, into an infantry slogging match with grenades and bayonets, while Hurricanes and Messerschmitts mixed it in the sky overhead and the Stukas had to be called off because the opposing forces were so close together in some places that it was impossible to tell exactly where the front line lay. After three hours Crüwell's task force had to withdraw, the British positions undented.

By this time, the leading elements of 21st Panzer Division, in the van of the southerly prong of the advance, were half way to Rafid, having encountered no opposition. Nehring therefore took the decision to halt them and detach the Panzergrenadier regiments from each division – the 6th, 7th, 104th and 115th – to assault the Allied positions from the rear up the Kuneitra road while the Panzers themselves continued on towards Damascus. Under more normal circumstances it would have been an extraordinary decision, because the whole concept of the Panzer division was the melding of tanks with motorised infantry and artillery. However, the remaining British forces in Damascus were known to be very weak, while winkling out an infantry position was a job for infantry, not armour.

From his command post in a rocky redoubt just outside Nafekh Field Marshal Alexander could see the German half-tracks toiling up the road towards Kuneitra to the north-east, blocking any possible line of retreat. Alongside him, General Freyberg looked haggard, his eyes like those of his men gritty and bloodshot. He had, after all, been in the front line for over a year apart from brief spots of leave and had not been home to New Zealand since shipping out in 1940.

'It looks like the game's up, Bernard,' Sir Harold Alexander said to his subordinate. Their combined forces on the heights numbered no more than 6,000 men now, fewer than a hundred field and anti-tank guns and a mere eighteen tanks. Against them was ranged the best part of four crack German divisions. 'Not without a hell of a fight,' his fiery New Zealand companion retorted. He was dead right. The Indians and New Zealanders fought until they ran out of ammunition for their Lee-Enfield rifles and their water-cooled Vickers machine-guns seized as a result of over-heating. The veterans of the Afrika Korps paid a terrible toll in blood for every rock and ravine. At one point a squad of the 104th Regiment was so pinned down by vicious crossfire that the men simply buried their heads in the hard, dry ground and refused to move . . . until their officer, Hauptmann (Captain) Wolf Wedemeyer, pulled the pin from a stick grenade and tossed it to the ground behind them. He commented afterwards while a nurse was stitching a nasty-looking but superficial gash in his forehead, 'You've never seen men move so fast!' It was a trick he had learned from the brawny Leibstandarte SS commander, 'Sepp' Dietrich. His men overran the Indian machine-gun position which had been giving them so much trouble and Wedemeyer received the Iron Cross, First Class.

In the end, sheer weight of numbers and the aerial onslaught prevailed. Cut off, short of ammunition, hot, tired and thirsty, the Allied troops were in an impossible position. If there had been any chance of a relief column reaching them, they might have endured for a few hours longer, but that chance had long since passed. They had chased the Italians half way across North Africa and been chased back in turn. With no avenue of retreat left open to them there was only one solution. Reluctantly, Alexander gave the order and the white flags started appearing.

Russian forces invaded Persia within days of the beginning of Operation 'Barbarossa', as Churchill had requested earlier, but it was a familiar story of 'too little, too late'. Once the last resistance in Palestine had been crushed, Syria and Iraq joined the Axis, thousands of volunteers crowding forward to join the Arab Legions of the Waffen-SS. The Royal Air Force managed to salvage most of its aircraft still in these countries and staged them south to Kenya, Tanganyika and Southern Rhodesia, packed to their gills with the few remaining soldiers and officials who had escaped capture and imprisonment. Nehring's Panzers, after licking their wounds and proudly pinning on their 'Golan 1942' armshields which had been authorised by a grateful Führer, now had the unaccustomed experience of driving over roads where they did not have to fear a surprise enemy attack from behind every other ridge. Jordan had declared itself neutral and, after some hesitation, Hitler had agreed to leave the kingdom alone . . . for the time being, at least. His eyes were now focused far beyond petty Middle Eastern states towards the riches of the Donets Basin, the distant Caucasus Mountains, the Maikop oilfields, and the cities of Rostov on the River Don and Stalingrad on the Volga.

Rommel's forces secured a passage over the Dnieper at Kremenchug, his pioneers labouring to get the pontoon bridges into position before a Russian counter-attack could dislodge the assault troops who had earlier crossed the river in inflatable boats powered by outboard engines. The expected riposte did not come, however. The Soviet high command was so shaken by the disaster at Uman that no-one was sure of the best course of action, and Timoshenko was still trying to pick up the pieces inherited from the unfortunate Budenny. At Dnepropetrovsk the Russian 13th Army fought more stubbornly and it was largely the efforts of the 'European' 5th SS Motorised Division *Wiking* which eventually secured a breakthrough and delivered the smouldering city into the Wehrmacht's hands. Felix Steiner, its commander and the man behind much of the esprit de corps in the Waffen-SS, was awarded the oak leaves to his Knight's Cross in commemoration.

Thus by the end of June the situation was broadly as follows. In the north, Leningrad besieged; in the centre, von Kleist's Panzers pushing at Smolensk; in the south, Rommel poised to capture Kiev and Guderian preparing to push on from Dnepropetrovsk; and in the Middle East, German troops celebrating in Damascus and Baghdad and rebuilding their strength again before venturing across the border into Persia. Unbeknown to them all, at the same time Walter Schellenberg was getting ready to disembark from his U-boat and preparing for his fateful meeting with the Duke of Windsor.

There was another fateful meeting of minds at this time between two equally unlikely men. Reinhard Heydrich, who had assumed Himmler's mantle as Reichsführer-SS after the latter's assassination in Prague, usurped Ernst Kaltenbrunner, the other front runner for the post. A far more intelligent man than either Himmler or Kaltenbrunner, he shared his subordinate Schellenberg's distaste for the Nazi regime's extremist racial policies, not from any moral or humanitarian principles but on the purely pragmatic basis that they were wasteful. The scar-faced Kaltenbrunner, who had vividly demonstrated his hatred of Jews in Austria after the *Anschluss* and had subsequently been given a post in Poland, was away from the centre of the action when Himmler was killed, which gave Heydrich a head start and, we can be sure, a lever or two to use against his Austrian opponent for the leadership of the SS, SD and Gestapo.

Heydrich, who himself privately feared that he carried Jewish ancestry in his blood – his mother's forename was Sarah and his father's surname Süss – had professed an anti-semitism which had, along with his aquiline Nordic good looks, endeared him to Himmler. Now, craftily working with rather than against the system, he befriended the National Socialist Party's sometime mentor and supposed intellectual, Alfred Rosenberg. The latter, author of the weird but influential book *Myth of the Twentieth Century* which had become a second 'bible' to *Mein Kampf* since its publication in 1930, had himself been born in Estonia and keenly felt that the people of the Baltic states – and those of the Crimea and Ukraine – shared more affinity with the 'Aryan' Germans than they did with their Russian (Slav) overlords.

This was a factor which the unscrupulous Heydrich, who was even feared by Göring (one of Rosenberg's chief detractors), could exploit to his own advantage. Gottlob Berger, in charge of Waffen-SS recruitment, had already achieved miracles in gaining volunteers from the European occupied countries such as Norway, Denmark, Holland and Belgium. Now, with Heydrich and Rosenberg – Party minister for foreign affairs – to support him, Berger could draw on the huge anti-Russian populations of the newly occupied areas to boost his own (and Heydrich's) regime. Between them they persuaded Hitler to withdraw the extermination squads, the *Einsatzgruppen*, from the lines of advance of Army Groups North and South apart from a token presence of men who were instructed to concern themselves solely with Jews, and to leave the rest of the people alone. These, Heydrich argued, and even Hitler listened, were Germany's natural allies. The Crimea, for example, was where the last pure Goths had died out in the 16th century. Rosenberg even suggested renaming it 'Gotenland' and Sevastopol 'Theodorichhafen' ('Theodor's Haven') after the Red Army had been driven out.

The Crimea was to become Germany's 'Gibraltar' on the Black Sea and a resettlement area for the Third Reich's ex-panding population. Russians would be forcibly moved out but

Tatars and Ukrainians allowed to remain . . . while it suited the Führer, of course. Himmler had advised postponing any such plan until after the war had been won, but the more dynamic Heydrich did not see why it should not be implemented the moment the Crimea was firmly in German hands. He thus gave influential support to Rosenberg's ideas, which up to this point had really been disregarded by most people as pipedreams. On top of everything else, the Crimea would provide an excellent home for the 2,000-odd non-Jewish Germans then living in Palestine. In the Ukraine, a great new university would be established and German would become a compulsory language in all schools.

Heydrich and Rosenberg found a further unexpected ally in Feldmarschall von Bock, who had been impressed by the generally favourable reception Army Group South's troops had received from the local populace, and had already issued standing orders that civilians should be treated as allies rather than as 'inferiors'. Agricultural quotas issued were to be as lenient as possible, supplies of consumer goods were to be maintained as nearly as circumstances permitted in pre-war fashion, schools and hospitals were to be kept functioning and religious freedom was to be respected. The last instruction applied only to Muslims and Orthodox Christians, of course, not to Jews, who would have to suffer the same fate as those in the rest of occupied Europe and be deported to the various concentration, slave labour and extermination camps. Bock's reasoning behind these orders, most unusual ones for a field commander to issue without reference to the politicians – which in this case would have meant Hitler himself – was that it would be foolish to antagonise people already halfway well disposed towards the German cause. There were enough Russians to be dealt with; why create additional enemies?

The plans did not work out entirely as hoped, because Russian nationalism ran high and Stalin was already calling the conflict the 'Great Patriotic War' in his own attempt to rally popular support against the invaders. Many Ukrainians, Tatars and men from the Baltic states therefore rallied to the partisan groups which had begun springing up within days of the invasion and had subsequently done a great deal of harm in attacking convoys and isolated troop outposts behind the front lines. The vast majority of people, as usual, remained indiffer-

ent and joined neither side. However, large numbers began
rallying to the Swastika as the SS recruitment programme
gained momentum.

In other areas of the Greater Reich, anyone wearing the
lightning rune insignia of the SS was regarded with suspicion,
hostility and fear. The combat troops of the four premier Waffen-SS divisions in Russia (1st, 2nd, 3rd and 5th) therefore
found it a welcome contrast to be greeted with smiles, offers of a
glass of milk and even other forms of hospitality which have for
eons been part of a soldier's 'perks'. True, there were incidents,
many of them wholly unpleasant. In one village troops from the
2nd SS *Das Reich* Division rounded up all the local Jews,
herded them into the synagogue then set fire to the building.
Those who tried to escape were gunned down mercilessly.
There was an enquiry into the affair, but it was hushed up and
no culprits were ever brought to justice. In some respects the SS
succeeded in remaining a law unto itself throughout the conflict. Such occurrences naturally caused resentment and fear,
but with the withdrawal of the *Einsatzgruppen* they were remarkably rare. As in Czechoslovakia, Heydrich was showing
that the age-old tactics of carrot and stick, especially when the
former was lavish and the latter sparingly applied, worked
genuine wonders.

As Guderian's Panzergruppe recovered its breath following the
fierce battle for Dnepropetrovsk, Rommel's tanks were swinging northwards towards Kiev, while down from the north returned Hoth's 'roving' Gruppe IV. There were two Soviet
Armies in the vicinity of the city, a force of some 300,000 men,
but by this time the Wehrmacht was used to dealing with
hitherto inconceivable numbers. Timoshenko, seeing the line
of the River Dnieper now breached in two places, had wanted to
withdraw eastwards, leaving the city open while he prepared
for a counter-attack, but Stalin refused to change his instruction that Kiev must be defended at all costs. It was a fatal error.
The destruction of Kirponov's forces had left the defenders
virtually denuded of tanks, although they had plentiful numbers of artillery pieces, including light and heavy anti-aircraft
guns which took a fearsome toll of the Luftwaffe's bombers.
More than any army in the world, the Russian's still considered
artillery the principal arbiter of battle.

A dense pall of smoke rising from the rubble of the once beautiful city, visible for tens of miles, was the Panzer crews' first indication that they were nearing their goal. Then, all too soon, the earth began exploding all around them as the Russian gunners found the range. Hatches clanged shut and the tank crews braced themselves for the inevitable impact. The Panzergrenadiers, disembarking from their half-tracks, followed the tanks into action, crouching behind or alongside them to gain some measure of protection from the rain of fire, no matter how illusory. Now machine-guns and mortars began opening up as the range decreased. Stukas screamed from the sky, protected from the Red Air Force by waves of fighters overhead; one of the Messerschmitt 109s was piloted by a blond, Teutonic young Leutnant called Erich Hartmann, who would end the war as the Luftwaffe's – and the world's – leading scoring fighter ace.

As the Panzers and their supporting troops enclosed the city in a ring of steel and fire, the defenders fought back with increasing desperation. They could expect no relief, for Marshal Zhukov, who had now been recalled to take over the defence of Moscow, could spare no troops of his own if he wanted to hold Army Group Centre at Smolensk. There, another great battle was in the offing.

The battle for Kiev lasted an exhausting eight days during which the soldiers of both sides got virtually no sleep. Their eyes gritty and bloodshot, they fought like automata, their gun barrels becoming red hot. Stretcher bearers rushed from one spot to another to take casualties back to the overflowing field hospitals where surgeons slithered on ground saturated with blood. Men waited hours in the scorching heat for attention, many succumbing to their wounds before they could reach the operating tables.

After five days Panzergrenadiers of General Werner von Erdmaunsdorf's 18th Panzergrenadier Division, part of Hoth's command, first penetrated into the city suburbs. From that point the battle assumed a different character, for Russian snipers and machine-gunners fired from every rooftop and window, or dug themselves into the rubble. Each strongpoint had to be winkled out individually. Eventually, however, Marshal Semyon Timoshenko could do no more. His troops everywhere virtually out of ammunition, he sent a courier with a white flag to Rommel. On 19 July von Bock flew in to formally

accept the city's surrender in the presence of Rommel and
Hoth.

The repercussions in the Kremlin were everything that
might have been expected, the members of the Politburo leaping up and down to accuse each other of treachery. Stalin was
practically foaming at the mouth. Only one man held his peace,
Lavrenti Beria. This mild looking, balding and bespectacled
man was head of the NKVD, the dreaded Russian secret police.
Amongst other perversions, his 'hobby' was having young
pubescent girls dragged in off the streets of Moscow to satisfy
his lust. Their parents would subsequently be bought off or, if
necessary, caused to 'disappear'. As far as Beria was concerned,
if the politicians blamed the army for the disaster it suited his
own plans well. So did any defeat which reduced the army's size
and effectiveness. The NKVD was as well armed as the army
and there had always been rivalry and antagonism between
the two powers. Beria was just biding his time before putting
the army in its place. Unknown to most people, Beria had since
pre-war days maintained close clandestine relationships with
Müller, head of the Gestapo, and more recently with Heydrich
as well. Such men have never really owed any loyalty to anyone
other than themselves.

After the fall of Kiev, the fighting in the southern sector
quietened down and attention focused on the centre, where von
Kleist was approaching Smolensk. Here, Zhukov had managed
to assemble three fresh mechanised Corps which were determined to prevent the invaders getting any closer to Moscow.
Here, too, Zhukov was also determined that the Germans
should not encircle his forces as they had done around Uman.
At the first sign of a breakthrough, his divisions would fall back
on Borodino, where a long ridge, protected for much of its front
by a steep-banked and fast-flowing river, afforded an excellent
defensive position. As it turned out, this contingency plan did
not need to be put into effect. Kleist's Panzers attacked with all
their usual skill and panache, and Smolensk was itself reduced
to a blazing ruin through which scurried the usual looters, but
this time the Russian tanks fought with suicidal courage and
although hundreds of them were destroyed, they halted the
Panzers' advance and forced them, greatly depleted, to retire
behind a defensive line established by the following infantry.
For the moment, it was stalemate on the central front, while

in the north the defenders of Leningrad still held out with fanatical stubborness.

Smolensk was the first major reverse the Wehrmacht had suffered and Hitler was furious, accusing his officers, just like Stalin, of cowardice and treason. He was only mollified by Schellenberg's news from Bermuda and was eagerly awaiting the arrival of the Duke of Windsor in Berlin, so did not demand von Kleist's resignation, normally his usual answer to an unsuccessful General.

The powerful locomotive rattled across the steppes towing a long train of flatbed cars. On these rested the monstrous, squat shapes of the first Company of the new Tiger tanks. They formed part of the 501st schwere Panzer Abteilung (1st heavy Tank Battalion), an independent formation not attached to any of the Panzer divisions but available for disposition at Korps level. The new tanks were so large that they could not fit on standard German railway wagons, so for rail transport the mudguards and outer set of interleaved roadwheels had to be removed and special narrow sets of tracks fitted. On arrival at their destination – in this instance Kiev – they then had to be offloaded and their wheels and road tracks replaced before they could be sent into action. However, they were formidable vehicles and even though as yet there were comparatively few of them, they would prove invaluable to von Bock in exploiting the advantages secured by Hoth, Rommel and Guderian.

Each tank weighed over 50,000 lb and had frontal armour up to 110 mm thick. Their main feature, though, was the 88 mm gun, a modified anti-aircraft weapon fitted with a muzzle brake to reduce the immense recoil. With a muzzle velocity of 2,657 feet per second, this could knock out any Russian tank at 1,000 yards or more and was to come as quite a shock to the Red Army, who would find its own guns incapable of denting a Tiger at the same sort of ranges. The Tiger was powered by a Maybach V-12 petrol engine which gave it a top speed of 24 mph, and its crews expected great things from it.

The train arrived at the heavily bomb-damaged marshalling yards in Kiev on 2 August to a reception committee which included Rommel and Hoth, both keen to see this latest addition to the army's inventory. They clambered over the vehicles like schoolboys, asking their crews excited questions and quite oblivious to the damage they were inflicting on their carmine-striped breeches. Both men had been at the prototypes' demonstration earlier in the year, but these were working production models, factory fresh in their muddy yellow paint scheme and as yet practically undented despite their thousand mile train journey.

'This'll sort a T-34 out!', Hoth exclaimed, slapping the solid steel side of one of the new tanks. Even though the latest generation of Panzer IVs were emerging from the Krupp, Steyr and Vomag factories with long-barrelled 75 mm guns and extra armour plating, with further improvements still in the pipeline, the Wehrmacht badly needed a tank which was better than its adversaries, rather than merely an approximate equal.

The two men continued to watch in fascination as the link pins were knocked from the travelling tracks and the wider road tracks were rolled into place. Then each tank's powerful engine bellowed into life with large puffs of black smoke through the exhausts and they began rolling forward with a metallic rattle and squeak, commanders smartly throwing salutes from their turret cupolas. Von Bock wanted to throw them straight into the front line, but Rommel and Hoth argued persuasively that it would be much better to wait until the whole Abteilung had arrived, so that the Tigers could be committed in strength rather than piecemeal.

Meanwhile, Georg Meier was soldiering on with his Panzer III, repaired time and again after breakdowns and hits, and still bearing the legend 'One Eye' even though its headlamp had long since been replaced. It had become a lucky tank, a talisman for the Troop, the vehicle and its young commander seemingly indestructible. He was now heading ultimately for Rostov-on-Don, his body inured to the constant pitch and roll of the tank over the dusty, unpaved roads, his mind no longer registering the hiss and crackle in his earphones but alert to the first word of an order. He had lost weight – they all had – but what was left was pure gristle. It needed to be.

Guderian's Panzergruppe, advancing on the right of the armoured spearhead through Donetsk with Rommel's Panzers to its north advancing via Lugansk almost directly to Stalingrad further east, and Hoth's beyond them in echelon formation basing their line on Kharkov, brooked no resistance.

The tanks spun on their tracks as they wheeled in a synchronomy born of experience and rigorous training. Their gunners had learned to pick up the elusive dot of a target through the obscuring smoke and dust and fire by instinct as much as by aiming. Their drivers had learned how to take advantage of every sheltering nuance of terrain which would protect or give a better firing position. They worked as a team, both within the tank and between the tanks in the Troop, and between them and the rest of the Company. The orders which had to be issued became fewer and fewer as the men learned to understand instinctively what was expected of them, and operated together almost as though by telepathy.

On the southern front the German line-up seemed impressive: eight Panzer divisions plus the elite *Großdeutschland* Division which was classed as Panzergrenadier but actually had as many tanks as a regular Panzer division; six motorised army divisions and the Waffen-SS's *Das Reich* and *Wiking*, which were also being upgraded; and the new heavy Tiger battalion with 59 tanks to create the effect of a butcher's cleaver through the Soviet defences. Plus the less mobile infantry divisions which, as usual, spent most of their time consolidating the ground taken and eliminating strongpoints of resistance bypassed by the Panzers. The total force was greater than that which had been used in the main attack on France in 1940. At the same time, Nehring's Panzer Armee Naher Osten had invaded Persia and was driving weak Russian forces back through the mountainous terrain towards Tabriz, close to the border with the Armenian Soviet Union. Beyond that lay Azerbaijan and Georgia, Stalin's birthplace; the oil port of Baku on the Caspian Sea, and then the Caucasus Mountains.

Georg Meier did not see much of the battle for Rostov and missed hearing the news of Britain's capitulation, which was greeted with jubilation by the rest of the army. He was in hospital. What annoyed him was that he didn't even have an honourable scar and a wound badge to show off to the girls back home. He had passed out with heat prostration and was hooked up to a saline drip while seeming gallons of lime juice were forced past his lips. Thus he missed his crew's triumph in taking the first German tank across the river into the heart of the city proper. As he learned afterwards, though, the battle had been far from easy. On the front from Kharkov to Rostov, Voroshilov (transferred after Zhukov's appointment and Timoshenko's surrender of Kiev), had roughly three-quarters of a million men, nearly 5,000 tanks (albeit, many of them now totally obsolete) and over 9,000 guns. The resistance at Kharkov was particularly tough, and since Hoth had only two Panzer divisions under command compared with the three in each of the other two Panzergruppen, he had the worst time of all. The battle raged through the city and its environs, backwards and forwards for four days, first one side and then the other gaining a temporary advantage.

The Russians persisted in throwing away their own numerical advantage, though, despite the arrival on the southern front of Marshal Fedorenko, Inspector General of Soviet armoured troops and Guderian's opposite number. When they did achieve a local breakthrough, they wasted it by haring off into the wild blue yonder, blindly seeking German headquarters and other behind-the-lines targets which they misconstrued as their main objectives, for the Russians had still not caught on properly to the aims and tactics of Blitzkrieg. When they stayed and punched it out, it was as isolated groups which could be disposed of in detail by the better co-ordinated Panzers. They also lacked the disciplined co-operation between the Panzer divisions' tanks and their supporting artillery and machine-gun equipped infantry, so the Soviets' own tanks were frequently isolated from their supporting arms and destroyed by skilfully disposed anti-tank guns. Most of the Russian tanks still lacked radios, which meant they had to operate in quite close groups so as to maintain visual contact. Finally, due to the enormous losses the Red Army had already incurred, tank crews were being thrown into battle with often only a few hours' training, in factory-fresh tanks which had not even been painted, such was the urgency of getting them into the front line. Thus it was that Hoth's numerically inferior but much more skilled and practised tank crews were able to secure advantage after advantage, withdrawing tactically when appropriate to draw the Russian armour onto the anti-tank guns, then riposting, refuelled and re-armed, when the Russians were literally at the end of their tether.

The situation was much the same at Rostov, although here the battle lasted a full week because the Panzergruppe had to keep its eyes on the strong Russian forces still holding around

Taganrog, on the Black Sea coast, and could not fully commit itself until 11th Army's infantry arrived to contain the threat to its southern flank. The end result was the same, though, and eventually Rostov was secured by the 20th of the month. Meier rather sheepishly rejoined his crew and dutifully admired the fresh dents in its battered superstructure from new hits.

Meanwhile, in the centre of the three Panzergruppen, Rommel – reinforced by the Tiger tank battalion – had made astonishing progress. The new tanks acted just as planned, although breakdowns were frequent through dust getting into the engines despite the special air filters with which they were fitted. Rommel's first objective was Poltava, which had been bypassed during the drive on Kiev and had subsequently been reinforced quite strongly and was known to have at least one resident mechanised Corps, roughly the equivalent of two divisions, under the command of General Vassili Chuikov. Chuikov was a comparatively young and able Soviet tank commander who, more than most of his contemporaries, understood the principles of modern armoured warfare. What he lacked was Rommel's intuitive grasp, experience and speed of reaction. Rommel always acted on the principle that a decision taken at the right time – any decision, even if it later proved with hindsight to have been the wrong one – was preferable to a decision taken too late. Thus began, as it turned out, the final clash of Titans.

Chuikov was aware that Hoth was likely to be held up severely at Kharkov and thus posed no immediate threat to his northern flank. He was worried about Guderian to his south but reckoned that his mind would be so fixed on his own goal, and his trust in Rommel's ability sufficiently secure, that he would leave the Field Marshal to sort out his own problems. He was quite correct, but he had still underestimated Rommel as an adversary. Nor had he, of course, forseen the new Tiger tanks. Rommel committed these as a right echelon spearhead, supported by Panzer IIIs and IVs to their left and rear. The Tigers came as a complete surprise to the Russians, who were used to losses but also accustomed to seeing their T-34s blast German tanks at ranges outside their own ability to fire back effectively. When the boot was put on the other foot, and T-34s started brewing up before they had fired a shot of their own, the Russians began panicking and their tanks were left milling around in circles without any real idea of how to cope with the situation. A couple of talented Company commanders realised the problem, and that the only way to cope with it was to get in closer so they were no longer outranged. Thus once again the tank gun versus armour plate pendulum swung in the opposite direction, as it is virtually bound to do ad infinitum. But those Russian commanders who reacted promptly and in the right manner were in the minority, and the Tigers blew a mile wide hole in the Russian lines through which the supporting lighter tanks poured, firing at their opponents at the sort of ranges which made the disparity in equipment almost unnoticeable.

Chuikov rallied quickly, and tried to launch counter-attacks to cut off the German spearhead, as had happened to so many Soviet formations. But with the poor communications and co-ordination already noted, his task was really hopeless and Rommel, the master of improvisation, was able to run rings around his armoured brigades. At the end of the day Chuikov had no option but to give the order to withdraw, especially since Guderian had now reached Donetsk and could have turned north to trap him. A running battle ensued, Rommel sensing Stalingrad almost within his grasp and determined to give Chuikov no time to regroup. The only modern parallels were Wavell's chase of the Italians back into Tripolitania in 1940-41 and Rommel's own rout of Eighth Army back across the same ground.

Chuikov turned at bay at Lugansk, on the River Donets, but after a hard battle found himself pinned against the river with inadequate bridges to allow his armour to escape. Abandoning thousands of his men along with hundreds of trucks, guns and tanks, he salvaged what he could and reformed on the eastern bank. Although his engineers had succeeded in placing demolition charges on the bridges, one was assaulted before they could be set off by the reconnaissance battalion of the *Das Reich* Division under Fritz Klingenberg (who had won the Knights Cross for his audacious capture of Belgade the previous year). Then the Luftwaffe held the Russian armour at bay while Rommel established a secure bridgehead and began concentrating his own tanks for the breakout towards Stalingrad, now only some three hundred miles away.

After capturing Rostov, Guderian had to pause again to allow supplies to catch up, together with infantry to secure the city and environs, before he could move again. Most of his own tanks were in a sorry state after their long forced march and breakdowns were becoming more and more common. Keitel and the OKW had predicted that the campaign would be over in nine or ten weeks and now, as the August heat reached its zenith, the Panzers were beyond that deadline. The campaign was now a race to crush the Russian will to resist before the Panzers could, literally, advance no further.

8
Interlude II

August in Berlin.

The linden trees were dusty but the pavement cafes were full and the streets were packed with cheering crowds, welcoming the news that the bombers of the Royal Air Force would not be dropping their deadly loads that, or any future night. Word of the British capitulation had just been broadcast. All right, the army was stalemated in northern Russia, but everything seemed to be going according to plan in the south. The main thing was that Britain – and hence presumably the rest of the Empire – was out of the running.

The abdication of King George VI caused a world-wide furore. One of the least sensible questions debated was whether Edward, Duke of Windsor, would be reinstated as the eighth king to bear that name or, since there had now been an intervening reign, the ninth. And should his wife, Wallis *née* Simpson, be the Queen, Princess Consort, Princess Regent (hang on, can a woman be a Regent?), or what should she be called? The Royal College of Heralds demanded an emergency debate on the issue, but whatever their deliberations might have produced was overruled by a decision handed down from Berlin. 'The lady is my wife. You have accepted me as your King once again. She is my Queen.'

This, quite apart from natural consternation at Britain's sudden and unexpected collapse, provoked even more discussion in America than in England. If she was Queen Wallis, didn't that mean that America now ruled England? That was the question yellow cab drivers in New York were asking, anyway. Behind the scenes, there was more serious debate. Those who had favoured bringing America into the war wholeheartedly on the side of England were now quietened. Without the island base of Britain to launch it from, any invasion to free the continent of Europe from German rule was out of the question. Conversely, those who had argued for American isolationism in the conflict were buoyant. America would not now be dragged into a second war to fight England's battle.

The news of the armistice was greeted with jubilation in Dublin, Madrid and Vichy, and both the Irish and Spanish governments promptly threw away their previous neutral stance and voted almost unanimously to join the Axis alliance. Ireland would be free at last of British apron strings and repression to develop in her own fashion. The Orangemen could be deported to the country they had so long bloodily supported, and at a stroke the real and imagined injustices of centuries could be rectified. Spain would again have control of Gibraltar. The latter was an issue which had both tempted Franco to join Hitler earlier, and had simultaneously kept him out of the war because the cost in lives and money of a siege would have been prohibitive against such elaborate, deep-sunk fortifications. Now that problem was also resolved by the stroke of a pen. The Vichy government demanded that de Gaulle and the other Free French leaders be returned to France to stand trial for treason. In the occupied countries the Resistance movements withered and died, for without the support of SOE, the Strategic Operations Executive, they could not hope to function effectively and all hope of a second front to liberate them had now disappeared.

In Australia, Canada New Zealand and other Dominion countries still loyal to the Crown there was heated debate. To which King did they now owe allegiance? George or Edward? This was still being debated hotly in parliaments, press and public houses when a new factor intervened.

On 7 September 1942 Japanese air and naval forces struck a devastating blow at the major American naval base of Pearl Harbor, Honolulu.

War between Japan and the United States had been brewing for years. Japan's expansionist policy had shown itself in Manchuria in 1931 and in an unprovoked invasion of China six years later. America severed trade relations in 1939. Then, in 1940 the Washington Naval Treaty expired. This had been drawn up after the First World War and limited maximum warship tonnages. Now Japan could start building the new battleships for which plans had already been laid down in anticipation. Next, following the fall of France, Japan (with the backing of German pressure) forced the Vichy French government to permit the occupation of northern Indochina, and in July 1941 of the southern half of the country as well. In the meanwhile, in April, even though a member of the Axis since the previous September, Japan signed a non-aggression treaty with Russia. It was obvious that a Pacific war was in the offing, but beyond freezing all Japanese assets, the United States still buried its head in the sand, hoping all would blow over.

Through all this period the Americans and Japanese still maintained diplomatic relations and talks continued between American Secretary of State Cordell Hull and Ambassador Admiral Kichisaburo Nomura, encouraged by the Premier, Prince Konoye. Hitler was incensed at the beginning of these talks and strong pressure was applied to persuade Japan to break them off, but wiser heads in both countries pointed out the advantages of keeping America neutral and off balance, at least until England was knocked out of the war. It was hard though to repress the War Party in Japan, led by General Hideki Tojo and Admiral Isoroku Yamamoto, who were following the German campaign in North Africa and the Mediterranean with intense interest while simultaneously looking greedily at the oil and mineral rich East Indies. On 16 October 1941 a military junta led by Tojo toppled the Konoye government and began intensive planning for war. Now Hitler applied pressure in the opposite direction, and instead of encouraging them, begged them to delay. The Royal Navy was still a formidable opponent and could severely hamper Japanese operations, but Britain could not hold out much longer, he said.

In fact Britain held out longer than anyone had expected and when Germany attacked the Soviet Union in May 1942 Tojo was only persuaded with enormous difficulty not to launch a pre-emptive strike against America immediately. Once Britain capitulated in August, though, he let leash his dogs of war, in particular the magnificent navy which Yamamoto had built up.

British warships at sea at the time of the armistice were ordered to return to port. Some refused, including the battle-cruiser *Renown* and the brand-new battleship *Prince of Wales*, which put into Sydney. It was a strange sight to see British and Japanese warships at anchor together at Singapore and Hong Kong, and soon they would be joined by German vessels too. The *Bismarck* had been sunk in 1941, of course, but now the battleship *Tirpitz* emerged from its Norwegian fjord to sail to the Black Sea and take part in the bombardment of Sevastopol, while the battlecruisers *Scharnhorst, Gneisenau* and *Prinz Eugen* sailed for the Indian Ocean. German U-boats too, apart from those needed to maintain a blockade of the United States' eastern seaboard, could also be released for Pacific Duty.

The blow when it fell still rocked America and almost resulted in President Roosevelt being impeached. For the attack on Pearl Harbor Admiral Yamamoto had assembled a fleet of six carriers, the *Akagi, Kaga, Shokaku, Zuikaku, Hiryu* and *Soryu*, with an escort which included two modern battleships plus light and heavy cruisers and a screen of destroyers. Their aircraft were the most modern naval designs in the world, and included the fast and manoeuvrable Mitsubishi Zero fighter, Kate torpedo bombers, Val dive bombers and Zeke long-range escort fighters. In Pearl Harbor on the 7th were the American fleet carriers *Enterprise* and *Lexington* and the battleships *Arizona, Nevada, Oklahoma, West Virginia, California* and *Tennessee*. All was quiet. No alert sounded.

The Japanese fleet, commanded by Admiral Chuichi Nagumo aboard the *Akagi*, approached the Haiwaiian group of islands undetected during the night of the 6th/7th. Well before dawn the ships were 250 miles from Pearl, steaming into the wind at 26 knots. Aircraft engines were warmed up and one by one they were catapulted into the clear blue vault of the sky, to circle and assemble and then head south for their target. Because of the numbers of aircraft involved, they could not all be ranged on deck at the same time so had to be launched in two waves an hour apart. The first wave, led by Commander Mitsuo Fuchida, comprised 183 Kates, Vals and Zekes; the second, led by Lieutenant-Commander Shimazaki, comprised a further 170 aircraft.

As the sun rose, Fuchida's force flew over a placid, glittering blue ocean. There was no sign of American aircraft. Apart from a few bored watchmen, the majority of American sailors and airmen were still sleeping as the Japanese aircraft crossed the coastline just before 6 am. Fuchida broadcast the signal Admiral Nagumo had been hoping for: 'Tora, Tora, Tora!', meaning that their surprise was complete. They had, in fact, been tracked by radar but were assumed to be US Army Air Force B17 Fortress bombers out on an exercise so no alarm was sounded. Then the Kate torpedo bombers were roaring at low level towards the serenely moored warships. The Americans still had not installed anti-torpedo nets in the harbour and the ships were sitting targets, too big to miss. Overhead more Kates armed with 1,760 lb armour-piercing bombs began dropping their loads as well.

The thinly armoured carriers suffered the worst damage, their enormous hulls forming irresistible targets for the torpedoes while their flight decks, unlike those on British carriers, were also unarmoured and the bombs plummeted straight through into the ships' vitals. Two torpedoes struck the *Lexington*, three the *Enterprise*. They were already listing and starting to sink rapidly when a rain of bombs blew their guts out. Huge explosions threw tons of metal high into the air and raging fires broke out. Within moments there was little left.

The more heavily armoured battleships fared only slightly better. One bomb penetrated right through to *Arizona's* forward magazine, and a gigantic explosion severed the ship's bow, pulling her rapidly down to the mud of the harbour floor. Black, oily smoke rose hundreds of feet into the air. *Oklahoma* was struck by five torpedoes and capsized. *West Virginia* almost suffered the same fate but quick thinking officers opened the sea cocks so counter-flooding kept her upright as she sank, her masts and superstructure projecting above the surface of the water. The harbour filled with oil and frantically swimming men trying to escape the carnage. Aboard the remaining ships, a few anti-aircraft guns were beginning to open up as the Val dive bombers arrived to add their 500 lb bombs to the destruction. Then, suddenly, the skies were clear. Hundreds of men had died, either immediately from blast or more horribly from fire or drowning.

Half an hour later Shimazaki's second strike wave arrived, but by this time the defenders were fully alerted and they ran into a massive barrage of anti-aircraft fire. While the first wave had suffered only half a dozen aircraft shot down, Shimazaki

lost forty. But they succeeded in completing the damage, blow-
ing up the *Pennsylvania* in dry dock and sinking two more
cruisers. When they finally departed and silence settled over
the stunned harbour apart from the crackling of flames, cries of
the injured and shouts of the fire-fighting crews, the pride of the
American Navy lay in shattered ruins. America had paid the
penalty for thinking she could stay out of the war and the world
would never be the same again.

9
Final Solution

Hanna Reitsch lay strapped in the tiny capsule in a state closer to terror than anything she had ever experienced in over a decade of test flying new aircraft. From light aircraft and gliders to the latest prototype fighters, it was all one to a professional who had already won international awards for duration, distance and altitude records in the 1930s. She had test flown an early version of the Fieseler Fi 103 pulse jet aircraft, designed to be launched as an unmanned flying bomb against England before that country's collapse. She had also been closely involved throughout with the rocket programme at Peenemünde, and had been scheduled to help in the test programme of the Messerschmitt 163 Komet rocket-propelled interceptor which had now been cancelled.

A true child of the 20th century, Hanna Reitsch had been born in 1912 so was still only small when the First World War ended. In her teens she had succumbed to two temptations – flying, and the magnetic personality of Adolf Hitler, to whom she gave a personal loyalty which was strangely reciprocated by the dictator who normally only awarded passing courtesy to women. It was a singular accolade to be sitting – or rather, lying – as she now was, but for brief moments Hanna wished she was anywhere else. 'Heini Dittmar should be here, not me,' she thought briefly, but poor Heini had injured his spine badly in a rough landing a couple of months previously and it was far from certain that he would ever be able to fly again.

The circular capsule rocked briefly as the gantry disengaged with a series of metallic thuds. Its white-painted metal interior was barren apart from a radio, barometric altitude and cabin pressure gauges, four buttons to control the attitude jets, a sealed red button to fire the retro-rockets, another to release the parachutes and an emergency one to blow the bolts which held fast the hatch behind her. Oh, there was a three-inch diameter porthole in front of her too, and a Zeiss camera firmly strapped in place beside her seat. The rest of the space was occupied by two oxygen bottles and a carbon dioxide 'scrubber'.

Wernher's voice rasped in her earphones. 'Two minutes, Hanna.' She pressed the 'acknowledge' button. No-one knew whether she would actually be able to speak during the fierce thrust of acceleration, so this little device on the arm of her seat enabled her to let those sitting safely in the concrete bunker know that she was still with them. The Führer himself was there, of course, along with Göring and every other member of the Nazi hierarchy who could wangle a seat. Hanna's attention was focused on Wernher von Braun, though, her flight controller and really the man who had made the whole mission possible. They shared a dream, and now that the dreadful war seemed almost over, it was within their grasp. How she hated the necessary indignity of the catheter and other plumbing attached to her nether regions, though.

The capsule in which she lay formed part of the nose cone of the modified A-4 (V-2) rocket which itself formed the second stage of the massive A-10 (V-3) lying beneath her, fuel tanks overflowing with Visol and nitric acid propellants. The A-4 had been designed to reach London from sites in Holland and northwestern France, rising roughly sixty miles in a ballistic trajectory to deliver a warhead just over 2,000 lb in weight at a speed of some 1,800 mph – fully supersonic and therefore virtually indetectable. After a number of failures, the design had been finally proven in the spring of 1943 with a series of test launches into the Baltic. But a rocket with a range of only just over 150 miles as the crow flies was of no use over transatlantic distances now the only real remaining enemy was America.

Following their devastating attack on Pearl Harbor on 7 September 1942, Japanese forces had made rapid progress in the Philippines and elsewhere. They had invaded Thailand from Indochina and Malaya at Kota Bharu, where British troops were uncertain how to react with Singapore already under the rule of a German military governor. The Indian forces present faced no such dilemma. If England was no longer their

protector, they had to fight for themselves. Many individual
English soldiers joined them. After the Yanks had finished the
Japs off, they could go home and sort out Hitler, couldn't they?
A shame about Pearl Harbor, but the good old US of A had
plenty of other ships, didn't it?

The Japanese assault was so swift that it was reminiscent of
the German Blitzkrieg through France and the Low Countries
in 1940. The main thrust was in the Philippines, where initial
landings were made at Batan on 9 September and Luzon two
days later. The American Far East Air Force was decimated,
its P-36 Mohawks, P-39 Airacobras, P-40 Warhawks and F2F
Brewster Buffalos being no match for the agile Zeros. There
were a few of the superior Grumman F4F Wildcats but none of
the new F6F Hellcats had yet reached the front line, so for the
Japanese pilots it was a 'turkey shoot'. Moreover, the loss of the
Enterprise and *Lexington* had left the American Pacific Fleet,
commanded by Admiral Chester Nimitz, totally lacking in carriers until the others – *Hornet, Long Island, Ranger, Saratoga,
Wasp* and *Yorktown* – could be brought back from the Atlantic.

At the same time that Luzon was attacked, part of the Pearl
Harbor task force, including the carriers *Soryu* and *Hiryu*,
were taking part in an amphibious assault on Wake Island,
which was defended by just a single battalion of Marines.
Nevertheless, they put up one hell of a fight, sinking two
Japanese destroyers and shooting down over twenty enemy
fighters before their own last fighter was itself shot down on the
21st, the same day that Japanese reinforcements arrived and
overwhelmed the last resistance. Guam had already fallen a
week earlier. The invaders seemed irresistible. Sarawak
(Borneo) was invaded on the 22nd and neighbouring Brunei on
5 October, Balikpapan and Kendari, in the Celebes Islands, on
the 23rd, Makasar on 8 November and Timor on the 19th, the
vital port of Rabaul falling on the 22nd. In Malaya General
Yamashita's troops had forced a crossing of the River Slim
against determined Indian resistance and on 10 November entered Kuala Lumpur. Hong Kong was surrendered without a
fight, while British troops in Singapore itself had been
evacuated by sea to Australia before the Germans arrived.

It should not be thought that the Americans under the
energetic Nimitz were sitting totally idle throughout this
period. Midway Island was reinforced and destroyers based in

Timor had inflicted heavy losses on the Japanese invasion
ships before being forced to withdraw in the face of concentrated air attacks. There were many individual cases of
heroism. On 12 December, for example, one of the last ships to
escape from Singapore was the *Li Po*, an old Yangtse steamer
commissioned as an auxiliary in the the Royal Navy. She was
captained by a Volunteer Reserve Lieutenant, 'Tam' Wilkinson, who had never seen combat, and was armed with just a
single four-pounder 'pop gun'. When Wilkinson encountered a
Japanese convoy of transport vessels escorted by a cruiser and
a couple of destroyers in the Java Sea, he did not hesitate but
ordered full speed ahead and roared into the attack. His gun
was ineffectual and his ship was badly hit, but he sank one of
the transport vessels by ramming it. There were only ten survivors from his crew; Wilkinson was not among them.

Now the Japanese invaded Sumatra, airborne troops capturing the important oil refineries at Palembang on 13 December
and the main amphibious force landing the next day. Five days
later the Australian mainland was attacked for the first time
as bombers roared over Darwin. By this time, however, the
other American carriers had returned to the Pacific and Nimitz
could begin to think of regaining some measure of control.

If the Allies were faring badly in the Far East, Russia was in a
state of turmoil. Rommel's Panzers had broken through
Chuikov's lines early in September 1942, scattering them almost literally to the four winds in total confusion. Exploiting
the advantage, and relying on the footsore infantry divisions
following to protect his rear and, if necessary, his flanks,
Rommel had flogged his weary tank crewmen on, subjecting
himself to the same strenuous hours so as to permit the Russians no respite, no time to fall back and regroup for what could
have been an extremely dangerous counter-attack, so overstretched were his lines of communication. Stalingrad was the
goal to be seized at all costs before the first autumn rains and
then the winter freeze set in.

Guderian's tanks faced less of a problem, which was probably
a good thing after the mauling they had received first at
Dnepropetrovsk and then at Rostov-on-Don. The Soviet forces
facing them were weaker than those which opposed Rommel
and Hoth although there was always the possibility that troops

and tanks bottled up in the Crimea could be ferried across the Kerch peninsula to come in on their flank from the general direction of Krasnodar. Fortunately this threat did not materialise, so indecisive was the Russian high command, and while Rommel was forging east Guderian turned south from Rostov towards Maikop. Here, the Soviet 64th Army under General Shumilov had established a rough line between Krasnodar and Kropotkin, using riverine defences wherever possible although many of the watercourses had dried out in the fierce heat and the land had become a nightmare of cracked earth and sheer gullies which spelled instant disaster to an inexperienced tank driver. Fortunately for the comparatively few remaining German tanks, there was a railway line still mostly intact to carry them over the intervening miles. Frequent halts were still necessary to repair gaps blown in the line by the retreating Russian forces though.

Georg Meier and his crew enjoyed the change, sitting perched on their tank in the sunshine while the locomotive did all the work and the distant peaks of the Caucasus Mountains floated on the horizon, seemingly drawing no nearer despite the miles which passed under the train's wheels. An even more exotic sight was the occasional Bactrian camel, but the men soon learned to approach them with caution for they could spit foul-smelling green mucus with unerring accuracy. 'Shows what the locals think of us,' one wag remarked.

The tanks detrained at Tikhoretsk, some miles from the front and out of range of the Russian guns, and reformed in their marshalling areas, directed by the Feldgendarmerie and myriads of unit signposts nailed to telegraph poles. In the dust and heat there was immense confusion and many accidents. One irate SS Colonel berated a Panzer IV crew for driving right over his Volkswagen Jeep; the obliging army driver promptly reversed back over it to free the wreckage from his tracks, cheerfully waved and continued on his way. Some accidents were less funny, as when a Sergeant caught his shirt sleeve in another tank's tracks and had it neatly severed below the elbow as he was pulled over a return idler wheel. But gradually order emerged from the chaos and the weary divisions were formed up for the attack yet again.

In Persia, Nehring had pushed a weak Soviet garrison out of Tabriz and the Luftwaffe's engineers were already busy

rebuilding the primitive airstrip there to provide a forward
landing ground to support the next stage of the advance, up the
narrow, winding road north to Ordubad and through the pass
over the Alborz Mountains leading down into the coastal plain
of Azerbaijan. There, their immediate target was Baku. Once
the port and oil refineries had been secured, they could then
swing westward towards Tbilsi in Georgia and think about
linking up with Guderian's forces once they in turn had broken
through Shumilov's 64th Army and captured the town of
Maikop and its surrounding oilfields.

Hoth, having achieved his own breakthrough after the four-
day battle for Kharkov, was now heading north-east via
Belgorod towards Voronezh, his progress slow because the
Russians had reverted to their hit and run tactics rather than
allowing themselves to be pinned in formal battle. In the north,
Leningrad still held out despite the ring of German and
Finnish troops which completely surrounded the city. However, this was no battle in which tanks could play a particularly
useful role, so Höppner's Panzergruppe, with Manstein's and
Reinhardt's two Korps and the SS *Totenkopf* Division, was now
diverted south to join von Kleist at Smolensk.

Unknown to the Germans, however, Zhukov was preparing
his own counterstroke. Around Vyazma he was concentrating
under the very capable General Ivan Koniev a grand total of
seven Armies – the 5th, 16th, 30th, 33rd, 43rd, 49th and 50th –
which included eleven new Guards divisions. Unfortunately
the latter, although graced with the title 'Guards' in an effort to
inspire morale and encourage esprit de corps, were Guards in
name only and severely hampered by a lack of heavy equipment and machine-guns. Facing them von Rundstedt now had
46 divisions, including Höppner's and von Kleist's two Panzergruppen. Additionally, the as yet unproven 22nd, 23rd and
24th Panzer Divisions, no longer needed in France after the fall
of Britain, had been entrained for the east under the overall
command of General Günther von Kluge as Panzergruppe VI.
The 4th Company in each division's two tank battalions consisted of new Panzer IVs with long-barrelled 75mm guns which
would shortly prove their worth in no uncertain manner.

Zhukov and Koniev were still grouping their forces, many of
them green troops with no combat experience, when von
Rundstedt struck on 15 September. His men were comparatively

rested after a month out of the front line, a month during which many battered old tanks had been cannibalised to make others roadworthy and more had arrived from the factories to make good most of the earlier losses. Von Rundstedt knew that this battle was crucial, that he had to hold Zhukov's – and Stalin's – attention focused to prevent them diverting divisions to aid Chuikov and Shumilov in the south. Whether an actual break-through was possible he did not know, but he was determined to give it his best try.

Manstein, riding as usual in his SdKfz 251 armoured person-nel carrier, was in the van of the advance, surrounded by older grey-painted and newer yellow-painted tanks, all bearing their black crosses and white divisional markings, including the letter 'H' for Höppner. Reinhardt's divisions were on his left and slightly to the rear, von Kleist's to his right, while von Kluge's new divisions formed a mobile reserve. The angle of the thrust was just south of Vyazma, at the junction of the Soviet 43rd and 49th Armies.

This time the Panzers of Army Group Centre were not to be denied. Preceded by the familiar artillery barrage from guns and Stukas, while Messerschmitt 110s and Junkers Ju 88s used their cannon to strafe the infantry and trucks and Heinkel 111s and Dornier 217s unloaded their own bombs on more static targets, Höppner's and Kleist's tanks opened a huge breach in the Vyazma front, immediately swinging north to try to cut off Koniev's northernmost five Armies. The two isolated Soviet Armies fought with desperation to link back up with the remainder of the defenders and to close the gap through which the Panzers were pouring, but they were contained by equally determined resistance from the supporting German motorised infantry, including the 1st SS Division Leibstandarte *Adolf Hitler* and the Army's own premier formation, the *Groß-deutschland* Division. (These two formations were unique in that, in addition to their fighting quality, they were hand-picked to provide Hitler's own personal bodyguard battalions.)

The battle of Vyazma would have turned into a virtual re-play of Uman if it were not for Koniev's tactical skill. The Russians were still not used to the speed with which the Panzers acted together and responded to threats, despite the fact that the T-34 was a far superior vehicle in every respect to all German tanks except the Tiger (none of which had yet reached Army Group Centre although the 502nd and 503rd schwere Panzer Abteilungen had virtually completed working up). Thus, with von Kluge's new Panzergruppe to pin Koniev to his front, the veterans of the other divisions roared into the Russian hinterland, smashing opposition wherever it was met or, in practised fashion, bypassing static strongpoints for those following to mop up.

Koniev reacted to the threat with a speed and decision uncharacteristic of most Russian field commanders, and with Marshal Zhukov breathing down his neck ordered a counterattack to try to seal the gap in his lines and isolate the Panzers themselves from their supply lines and supporting troops. A mammoth tank battle involving over 1,200 vehicles on either side took place south-west of Vyazma on the 18th. There was little finesse on either side, just the brutal reality of kill or be killed, often at point-blank range as tanks crested ridges or turned the corners of woods to bump headlong into enemy formations. Blackened hulks and charred bodies littered the landscape creating a carrion stench which none who have smelt it can ever forget. The tinder dry grass itself caught fire in many places, and the tanks and armoured personnel carriers blundered blindly through the dense smoke.

The individual tank crews could gain no overall picture of the sprawling battle, had no knowledge of whether they were winning or losing. All they knew was the urgency of keeping red-rimmed eyes constantly searching for fresh targets. Even in the Korps and divisional headquarters the situation was unclear as reserves were committed to threatened sectors and other units retired to refuel and restock their ammunition. Radial-engined Focke-Wulf Fw 190 and Lavochkin La-7 fighter planes fought their own mêlée overhead, diving to strafe targets of opportunity. Gradually, however, the Panzers gained the upper hand and Koniev was forced to withdraw, trying to salvage as much of his seven Armies as possible. He conducted a skilful retreat, the most difficult of military operations, using his tanks to cover the withdrawal of the infantry and artillery, then ordering the tanks to fall back on the new lines before repeating the process. It was a nightmare game of leapfrog and despite all Koniev's ability tens of thousands of Russian soldiers were cut off before they could extricate themselves. Resisting doggedly all the way, the survivors fought to establish a new line further east, in front of Moscow itself, while all available reserves were rushed to the city's defence. Zhukov knew that if he could just hold on for another month, winter would come to his aid.

In the south Nehring crossed the Russian border at Ordubad on the same day that Guderian's Panzergruppe opened its new offensive against Shumilov's 64th Army on 19 September. To their north, Rommel was steadily pushing Chuikov back towards Stalingrad, while Hoth had reached Belgorod where his forces captured over 50,000 new prisoners. The Russian front was crumbling rapidly.

'Thirty seconds, Hanna. Starting countdown now.' Wernher von Braun's voice rang clearly in her headphones. '. . . Ten . . . nine . . .' The seconds were ticking away rapidly, echoed by her heartbeat. Eighty feet beneath her couch, powerful pumps began forcing the two volatile fuels into the combustion chambers of the six 67,000 lb thrust rocket engines of the A-10's first stage. '. . . Four . . . three . . .' A wisp of smoke began to emerge from the base of the missile, the largest ever built. In the reinforced command bunker half a mile away scientists and Party dignitaries alike held their breath as they peered through periscopes or watched the small television monitor screens. '. . . Two . . . one. Ignition!' A belch of flame emerged from the rockets. This was the first critical moment. If even one failed to ignite properly the missile would spin out of control and Hanna Reitsch would be a dead woman.

All six lights on the board were green. 'Lift-off!' The huge A-10 hung poised on a pillar of flame barely inches above the ground, as though loath to leave the surface of the Earth. The noise came through to the anxious watchers as something felt through their bones rather than heard. In the capsule Hanna felt as though she was being shaken to pieces by the fierce vibration.

Slowly, ever so slowly at first but then with rapidly increasing momentum the missile lifted itself clear of the last umbilicals connecting it with the ground. Its speed increasing by the second it now hurtled skywards, balanced on a long plume of fire, gyroscopes keeping it steady. Accelerating rapidly, it dwindled in the jubilantly cheering watchers' vision, tracked only now by powerful binoculars. Fifty seconds after lift-off, the six primary engines flared and died. Explosives sheared the connecting clamps and as the first stage separated, the ballistic cone which had shrouded the upper, A-9 stage for its passage through the denser lower atmosphere, opened out like the jaws of a crocodile and fell away. Then the A-9's single 67,000 lb engine flamed into life, propelling the missile from the 2,660 mph it had already attained upwards ever faster to just over 6,000 mph. This was insufficient, of course, to break free of the tyranny of gravity or even to put the missile into minimum orbit, but by this time Hanna had reached a height of over fifty miles and the curvature of the earth was clearly apparent.

Now the capsule separated from the parent rocket which would continue to rise for a while, coasting, before falling back towards the Earth in a parabolic trajectory which would plunge it into the icy waters of the north Atlantic. Now, too, Hanna caught her first sight of the stars as they can never be seen from earth, burning steadily rather than twinkling. The capsule was tumbling slightly and she activated the compressed air directional jets to orientate herself so that she could see the Earth through the tiny porthole. From her altitude she was able to overlook practically the whole of Europe clear across to the British Isles. The English Channel looked absurdly narrow, hardly the barrier for an invasion force which it had proven to be. She could see the whole of the Danish peninsular and right across the Baltic into Scandinavia. Suddenly remembering, she took her camera from its fastenings. It nearly eluded her grasp and started to float away but she caught the carrying strap and began taking pictures. Far from being the nauseating experience she had half expected it to be, Hanna found the endless falling feeling of weightlessness positively exhilarating.

The capsule was actually beginning to fall now, although no movement was apparent from this height. However, if Hanna did nothing, she would follow the A-9 into the ocean, a prospect she did not fancy. Thus, turning the capsule so that her heat shield was now nose forward, she fired the retro rockets, producing a steady burst of pressure which once again pressed her into her contoured seat, though nowhere nearly as badly as on take-off. Soon she could hear the hiss as the capsule touched the tenuous uppermost layers of the atmosphere. The retro rockets had done their job and the capsule was now travelling at barely

4,000 mph. Atmospheric braking would take care of the rest, turning the heatshield cherry red.

Gradually the sky returned, deep indigo brightening slowly to blue. The capsule was cooling as it descended and at 15,000 feet the first drogue parachute opened. This slowed the swaying capsule still further until, at 10,000 feet it was safe to open the three main parachutes. Hanna saw she was descending over farmland in northern Denmark, her course tracked now by radar, and already Luftwaffe trucks were racing towards the projected touchdown point. Moments later the capsule landed with a sickening thump which threw Hanna against her seat straps. She was too lightheaded to care. For the first time man – or rather, woman – had ventured beyond the atmosphere into the vacuum of space. The whole mission had lasted barely twenty minutes – but no journey begins without the first step.

First steps were also being taken in another direction which was to produce from the A-10 the most potent weapon the world had ever seen. German scientists such as Otto Hahn, Fritz Strassmann and Paul Harteck had already determined the way in which uranium, bombarded by neutrons under controlled conditions, first captured some of the neutrons, then split and emitted more neutrons. In lay terms, the U235 nucleii began to 'fizz', and emit energy. This is the process known as nuclear fission and it was immediately apparent that the reaction could not only create a controlled form of very cheap power for the homes and industries of the Third Reich, but that utilised in a different way a 'critical mass' of uranium could form the core of a bomb a million times more powerful than any chemical reaction weapon. The term 'critical mass' refers to the quantity of uranium needed at one place and at the same time for it to start a self-sustaining reaction, without any outside neutron bombardment. This was far from an easy problem to solve, for means had to be devised of bringing together two sub-critical masses of the metal, themselves relatively inert, which would produce the desired chain reaction. Moreover, in the interests of gaining maximum output from the smallest amounts of uranium, it became apparent that they must be compressed hard and rapidly within a shell to enhance neutron bombardment and contain the reaction for a vital microsecond.

Following the fall of Britain, the rather desultory German research (whose only prominent supporter was Göring) was accelerated by the seizure of such places as the Harwell nuclear laboratory outside Oxford and the Cavendish laboratories in Cambridge, where pioneers in nuclear technology such as Cockcroft and Walton had worked in the 'thirties. By the time of the armistice in August 1942, the British scientists had outstripped the work of their opposite numbers in Germany and were closer to a solution of the problem. One particular 'catch' for the Gestapo was Klaus Fuchs, a German nuclear physicist who had fled the Hitler regime to work in England. The fact that he was a devoted communist sending regular reports back to Moscow escaped undetected by British security, but the Soviet Union had enough problems on its plate by this time and could not cope with the additional burden of a complex and expensive nuclear research programme. Another British scientist in a similar position was Allan Nunn May.

Both men had been working for the British research teams, with a limited degree of co-operation from the United States, since the end of 1941, and had a great deal of knowledge to impart. Their reluctance to co-operate was seen by the German occupying forces as nothing more than the general reluctance of the scientific community as a whole to share their secrets with their conquerors. Blackmail was the usual tactic employed by the Gestapo in recalcitrant cases. If nothing could be found to threaten the individual, then family, children and friends could always be used as levers. It is not known how much Fuchs, May and, undoubtedly others, managed to convey back to their original Soviet masters regarding the 'Brandenberg Project', as it was codenamed, for both died shortly after the end of the war, one in a car accident, the other from a house fire apparently caused by a burning cigarette end. Nor is it known what pressures were put on them, and several other scientists, to co-operate. Did the SD or Gestapo know their true loyalties all along and simply use them for their own purposes until they had outlived their usefulness? We shall probably never know.

The takeover of Britain provided other surprises for the OKW and myriad German intelligence services, not the least of which was Ultra, the closely-guarded decyphering centre at Bletchley Park which monitored and 'translated' all German signals encoded on the Enigma machines. This discovery came as a huge shock. Why had the British been so easily beaten if they had this crucial weapon to hand? Gradually the answers discussed earlier emerged. There was also a bonus: Britain had never shared the Ultra secret with the Soviet Union, so the armed forces could continue to use Enigma as usual. Introducing a new cypher system of comparable complexity at this stage in the war would have caused nightmarish problems.

The capture of British aircraft intact and complete instead of as thoroughly crashed or cremated wrecks also provided much valuable new technology. The Avro Lancaster bomber, which had first become operational in March 1942, would give the Luftwaffe a true strategic bomber superior to the He 177, with greater range and load-carrying ability. The de Havilland Mosquito would give them a long-range, high altitude reconnaissance and strike aircraft which could not be touched by anything either the Russians or, later, the Americans possessed. These also possessed far superior radar compared with anything the Luftwaffe had airborne at that time and excelled in the night fighter role. And of course there was the Spitfire, that superbly nimble little fighter which every Luftwaffe pilot yearned to fly. Now they would have their chance.

In Russia the advance had continued well until the onset of the rains in October caused everything to slow down as men, horses and vehicles bogged down in thick, glutinous mud. By this time Leningrad was in the fourth month of siege with no hope of a reprieve while the leading elements of Army Group Centre were within sixty miles of Moscow. The battleship *Tirpitz* with a strong destroyer escort had arrived on station in the Black Sea off the Crimean coast and was helping the army's railway artillery and enormous 'Karl' self-propelled siege mortars in reducing Sevastopol to rubble. In the south-east, Hoth had reached Voronezh and Rommel was at the gates of Stalingrad. A free Ukrainian Republic had been declared independent of Moscow rule, self-governing under German supervision. Latvia, Estonia and Lithuania had also declared for the Axis and were mobilising to throw their weight in with the Wehrmacht.

Meanwhile, Guderian had broken through Shumilov's line and thrown him back to the foothills of the Caucasus where the lie of the ground inevitably favoured the defence. The Panzers would be of little value here: it would be an infantry and artillery slogging match in which for the first time since Crete and Malta the highly trained *Gebirgsjäger* would come into their own. Julius Ringel's 5th Mountain Division had already been sent out to help Nehring's Panzer Armee Naher Osten force the passage of the Alborz Mountains, where they had been held up by determined resistance in the narrow passes as well as by the deteriorating weather, for they were not equipped to fight in snow. The other mountain divisions assigned to assist Guderian were the 1st under General Hubert Lanz, 3rd under Hans Kreysing, 4th under Karl Eglseer and 7th under August Krakau (the 2nd, 6th and 8th were still fighting with the Finns in the far north, where little progress had been made towards the capture of Murmansk because of the nature of the arctic terrain).

As mud turned to snow and ice the German advance halted completely. The cold became so intense that frostbite was a constant problem and there were many cases of sentries literally freezing to death during the bitter nights. Engine oils coagulated and cylinder blocks froze. The Luftwaffe did its best, flying out thousands of tons of supplies, the ex-RAF Lancasters playing a major part in this because they could reach the forward airfields from fields in Germany itself. There was a massive campaign at home to get women to knit for the troops, and uniform regulations were discarded in favour of warmth, fur or sheepskin coats and multi-coloured mufflers becoming the order of the day.

The Lancasters had other uses too. With their 1,600 mile range they could reach the factories the Russians had established 500 miles east of Moscow. Up to this point they had been considered invulnerable; now they rocked to the 'crump' of high explosive bombs (a Lancaster could carry a 14,000 lb load compared to the He 177's 4,400 lb) and the flare of incendiaries. Although the effects of this bombing campaign were small except in terms of their effect on Russian morale to begin with, they would rapidly become greater as the Luftwaffe crews became more used to their new machines. Nor was Soviet industry alone in feeling the weight of the Lancaster's power, for now Moscow began to suffer real air raids for the first time in the war, and although the city had the strongest anti-aircraft defences of any in the world apart from Berlin itself (and that had not stopped the RAF), still the bombers came night after night and the city's inhabitants prayed for heavy overcast to give them a respite. Unknown to them, German scientists were, using further finds in Britain, working on a new form of radar which would be able to 'see' through cloud and give the bomber crews a clear picture of the ground beneath.

Stalin had other problems elsewhere. In the Far East Japan, breaking the non-aggression agreement, had used North Korea as the springboard from which to launch an overland attack directed at the main Russian port on the Pacific coast, Vladivostock. Soviet divisions from Siberia, originally intended to reinforce Zhukov for a winter counter-offensive in front of Moscow, had therefore to be diverted to meet this new threat.

Elsewhere, too, the Japanese were continuing to make steady progress although it slowed as the distances increased and the Americans inflicted a severe defeat on them in the Coral Sea during February 1943. On the 4th of that month, the carriers *Yorktown* and *Hornet* under the command of Admiral William 'Bull' Halsey, rendezvoused with the cruiser *Chicago*, two Australian cruisers, *Australia* and *Hobart*, plus a destroyer escort. His task was to intercept a Japanese task force known to be heading south towards Port Moresby on the southern coast of New Guinea, an essential staging post for an invasion of Australia whose capture had to be prevented at all costs. American naval intelligence had provided details of the Japanese force's composition and course, because they had long since cracked the Japanese Purple Code in an operation comparable to Ultra. Although they did not know it, therefore, the Japanese ships were sailing into a well-planned trap.

There were three main elements in the Japanese force, sailing in separate convoys. First was the landing force, eleven troop transports escorted by six destroyers under Admiral Sadamichi Kajioka. Then there was the main covering group comprising the light carrier *Shoho* and four heavy cruisers under Admiral Aritomo Goto, and finally a strike force under Admiral Takeo Takagi with the two heavy carriers *Zuikaku* and *Shokaku*. On 7 February a reconnaissance aircraft from *Yorktown* excitedly reported sighting 'two carriers and four heavy cruisers'. Halsey assumed this was Takagi's main strike force and launched ninety-three Douglas Dauntless dive bombers and Devastator torpedo bombers. Unfortunately the

sighting report was wrong: the ships which had been sighted
were actually Goto's covering force with the carrier *Shoho*.
Goto's radar operators spotted the American aircraft approaching and launched some Zeke fighters, but they were overwhelmed and over a dozen bombs as well as several torpedoes
struck the carrier. 'Scratch one flat top', laconically reported
one Dauntless pilot. It was the first American victory over the
Japanese navy and a great boost to morale. Kajioka, in command of the virtually defenceless landing group, decided dis-
cretion was the better part of valour and withdrew to await
events.

Deteriorating weather prevented the Americans from spotting Takagi's ships that day and would have made an air strike
difficult if not impossible anyway, but battle was joined shortly
after dawn on the 8th, reconnaissance aircraft from both sides
spotting their enemy at virtually the same time. Takagi
launched his aircraft first but the Americans scored the first
blow. They did not spot *Zuikaku*, which was hidden beneath a
low cloud bank, but roared in on *Shokaku*. The attack was not
as successful as the earlier one on *Shoho* because the Japanese
flak was murderous and the torpedo bombers released their
weapons too early. Nevertheless, three dive bombers scored
hits causing fires in the carrier's bow which meant that although aircraft could be landed on, they could not be launched.
Takagi therefore ordered *Shokaku* to retire from the action.

Meanwhile Takagi's own air group, 69 Kates, Vals and
Zekes, had found *Yorktown* and *Hornet* basking under a cloud-
less sky. They launched a determined attack in which *Hornet*
was hit by two torpedoes and two bombs. At first the damage
was thought to be slight and the fires were quickly controlled,
but below the waterline it was actually quite severe and she
began to list. Water flooding in caused an electrical short-
circuit and a spark ignited petrol vapour deep in the vessel's
bowels. There were two large explosions and furious fires broke
out again. The ship had to be abandoned shortly after 5 pm.
Both sides then withdrew, honours roughly even, but it was
still the first real setback the Japanese had encountered.

Hanna Reitsch's historic flight was made on 12 April 1943, by
which time German forces had resumed their advance, reinforced by several new Tiger tank battalions as well as Panzer

IVs with long-barrelled guns. Zhukov had made one attempt at
a counter-attack during December, aimed at the joint between
Army Groups North and Centre, and although things had hung
in the balance for several days, it was finally repulsed. The lack
of the Siberian divisions had made itself felt. Now though, attention was refocused on the south. Rommel had made no effort
to try to take Stalingrad during the winter, wisely reckoning
that the defenders would have by far the best of things under
the appalling weather conditions. Now he struck again, using
his Panzers to encircle the city as had happened at Kiev. While
the tanks then formed an outward-facing ring to hold off the
inevitable relief attempt, the infantry and artillery slowly
crept forward, anti-tank guns holding off Chuikov's T-34s
which had a new weapon to face in the form of shaped charge
missiles launched by the German infantry from hollow metal
tubes. Called *Panzerfausts* ('armoured fists'), these weapons
only had a range of about thirty yards but could easily penetrate the T-34s' armour.

At the same time Guderian's mountain divisions were as-
saulting Shumilov's positions in the Caucasus and slowly
driving them back, while Julius Ringel's 5th Division had
succeeded in clearing a pass through the Alborz Mountains and
the 7th, 15th and 21st Panzer Divisions were on the rampage,
heading rapidly for Baku which was only comparatively
lightly defended. From there they could swing westwards so as
to come in on Shumilov's rear.

Oberst Walter Koch, hero of Crete and Malta, also found
himself with a new task at this time. Fearing that Stalin would
order the Maikop oilwells to be fired to deny them to the enemy,
Hitler had been persuaded by Kurt Student that his paratroopers
could seize the airfields in a surprise raid as the Japanese had
done at Palembang. This would also give Shumilov another
threat to worry about, so the 1st and 2nd *Fallschirmjäger* Divisions which had been formed from the earlier 7th Flieger Division and independent regiments were assigned the task. The
1st Division was commanded by General Richard Heidrich and
the 2nd by Bernard Ramcke.

The assault, at the beginning of May, almost the second
anniverary of the battle of Crete, went off textbook style, the
waves of Ju 52s disgorging their hundreds of parachutists in
wave after wave, followed by more of the lumbering transports

towing DFS 230 gliders with more infantry and quantities of
lightweight recoilless guns. The paras also had a new weapon
which was to prove highly effective, the FG 42 assault rifle, a
compromise between a rifle and a sub-machine-gun with the
accuracy of the former and high rate of fire of the latter. Although the Russian engineers succeeded in firing a few of the
wells, the remainder were captured intact. Germany's oil
supplies were now assured.

Stalingrad fell on 11 May and Nehring entered Baku two
days later. These further disasters, coupled with the Ukrainian
revolt, the intensified German bombing of Moscow and the
Ural industrial areas and the fact that Sevastopol could not expect to hold out for much longer, produced another crisis in the
Kremlin. Lavrenti Beria seized his chance. NKVD troops secured key positions throughout Moscow. A special task force
under a ruthless young commissar called Yuri Andropov broke
through the Kremlin guards into Stalin's study and riddled the
dictator with bullets. Beria assumed control of a terrified Politburo and declared his intention of suing for peace.

The Treaty of Moscow was signed on 1 June 1943, Hitler,
Ribbentrop, Göring, Heydrich and other top Party officials
flying in to Sherementevo for the ceremony with Beria signing
for the State and Zhukov for the army. It was remarkably
generous in some respects. Russian autonomy as a self-governing state but responsible to Germany for foreign policy was the
main point. The Red Army was to be reduced in size to no more
than twelve divisions and in time of war was to fall under
German command. The independence of Estonia, Latvia,
Lithuania, the Ukraine, Azerbaijan and Georgia was con-
firmed. All Russians living in the Crimea were to be relocated
and the peninsula was to be resettled by Germans. Germany
was to have first option on all surplus grain, if any. The war in
Europe was over. Only America remained.

Sarah Rosenberg looked dully at the strange new tower the SS
were building in the middle of the camp, miles from civilisation
deep in the Polish countryside. Her body shrunken from a star-
vation diet, bruised from the attentions of the coarse and brutal
guards, she regarded the world with total apathy after two
years in a variety of concentration camps. Yet she was one of
the lucky ones. She was still alive. It was warm in the sun and

she sat outside the hut watching the German engineers at work. The tower was much taller than the watchtowers around the camp, and there was a strange metal construction at its top over which white-coated technicians were sweating. Still, it was none of her business. Camp inmates learned early to keep themselves to themselves and avoid attracting attention.

The following morning the camp population awoke to a strange silence. There was no dawn roll-call and body count. Hesitantly the emaciated Jews peered from the doors of their huts. Where were the guards? There was not a German uniform in sight. Although the camp gates were barred, there were no machine-gunners in the watchtowers.

Those who happened to be looking at the tower in the centre of the camp may have briefly seen an intense white glare before their bodies were vapourised. A huge fireball expanded fiercely over central Poland, blast rings clearly visible to the observers in the heavily protected blockhouse ten miles away. Gradually an evil-looking mushroom-shaped cloud rose thousands of feet into the air. German scientists had succeeded in detonating the world's first atomic device, a two kiloton yield bomb. Using the camp as a focus and the isolated Polish farmhouses around as guinea pigs to determine the extent of the devastation caused had been Hitler's own idea – his final solution.

Three months later a modified A-10 rocket lifted off from the missile research establishment which had been created on the isolated Goonhilly Downs in Cornwall, England. High over the Atlantic it soared, the A-9 separating successfully from its first stage and covering the two thousand-odd miles to its target in minutes. The guidance was not perfect but a second mushroom cloud blossomed over Long Island Sound, incinerating Bridgeport and sending a huge tidal wave as far inland as New Rochelle. As a stunned American public listened to the incredible news later in the day all traffic stopped in the streets. Germany had issued President Roosevelt an ultimatum. Surrender, or one new city a week would be destroyed in the same way.

The American nuclear programme under Dr Robert Oppenheimer was months away from achieving a comparable capability. The American government had no choice. The Treaty of Tokyo was signed on 1 December between America, Japan, Australia and Germany. All American assets abroad were to be seized as war reparations, including businesses in South America. Australia as well as all the East Indies, Indochina, Burma, Wake Island, Guam and Midway were to become Japanese possessions. Perhaps the most mortal blow was the loss of Hawaii.

Walter Koch was celebrating with some of his men in a bar in Tbilsi, the sweet Georgian wine flowing freely, as the young Panzer Major strode in. 'Have a drink,' Koch offered hospitably. 'The war's over.' Georg Meier, who had also survived, offered a toast. 'The Führer!'

Index

INDEX